UNDERSTANDING *Our* EVANGELICAL NEIGHBORS

UNDERSTANDING *Our* EVANGELICAL NEIGHBORS

RICHARD J. MOUW
& ROBERT L. MILLET

CFI

An imprint of Cedar Fort, Inc.

Springville, Utah

© 2024 John A. & Leah D. Widtsoe Foundation
All rights reserved.

No part of this book may be reproduced in any form whatsoever, whether by graphic, visual, electronic, film, microfilm, tape recording, or any other means, without prior written permission of the publisher, except in the case of brief passages embodied in critical reviews and articles.

This is not an official publication of The Church of Jesus Christ of Latter-day Saints. The opinions and views expressed herein belong solely to the author and do not necessarily represent the opinions or views of Cedar Fort, Inc. Permission for the use of sources, graphics, and photos is also solely the responsibility of the author.

Paperback ISBN 13: 978-1-4621-4695-6
eBook ISBN 13: 978-1-4621-4783-0

Published by CFI an imprint of Cedar Fort, Inc.
2373 W. 700 S., Suite 100, Springville, UT 84663
Distributed by Cedar Fort, Inc., www.cedarfort.com

Library of Congress Cataloging Number: 2024931628

Cover design by Shawnda Craig
Cover design © 2024 Cedar Fort, Inc.

Printed in the United States of America
10 9 8 7 6 5 4 3 2 1
Printed on acid-free paper

Contents

Foreword   vii

Introduction   ix

SECTION 1: EVANGELICAL BELIEFS AND DOCTRINES

1. Evangelicalism: A Brief Historical Account	3
2. General Overview of Evangelical Beliefs and Doctrine	11
3. Beliefs in Common with Latter-day Saints	25
4. Areas Where Latter-day Saint Beliefs Differ	29
5. Appreciation for Evangelical Beliefs	35

SECTION 2: EVANGELICAL RELIGIOUS PRACTICES

6. General Overview of Evangelical Religious Practices	41
7. Practices in Common with Latter-day Saints	55
8. Areas Where Latter-day Saint Practices Differ	63
9. Appreciation for Evangelical Practice	69

SECTION 3: INTERFAITH DIALOGUE

10. Latter-day Saint Engagement with Evangelicalism	75
11. Appreciation for Latter-day Saint Beliefs and Practices	81

APPENDICES

Glossary of Evangelical Terms	87
Prominent Evangelical Figures	93
Suggested Readings	96
About the Authors	98

Foreword

This project grew out of a statement from Elder Dieter F. Uchtdorf about an article in a German newspaper telling its readers what Mormons believe. "They ought to ask us to tell their readers what we believe," he remarked. That got me thinking: Why not ask a scholar of another faith to write a short booklet about their religion, tailored for a Latter-day Saint audience? Then, why not ask a Latter-day Saint scholar to join in writing the booklet to show what this means to Latter-day Saints, what our commonalities are, and how and why we differ? This way, our work will be accurate from both traditions.

The outreach of The Church of Jesus Christ of Latter-day Saints over the past decade has been remarkable. As it continues to expand the world's understanding of its doctrine, mission, people, and culture, its membership is growing across the globe. This means that the Church's "neighbors" are becoming ever more diverse in their beliefs, lifestyles, and ways of worship.

Asking the world to understand the Church and its people must be accompanied by asking our members to also understand our neighbors, friends, associates, and communities so that we are better neighbors as well. This presents a great opportunity for the John A. & Leah D. Widtsoe Foundation to fulfill its mission to serve as the Center for Global Latter-day Saint Leadership and Life in a very real and meaningful way by presenting this *Understanding Our Neighbors* series.

It is one thing to learn to tolerate one another, but it is even more important to understand and ultimately to appreciate one another—our similarities as well as our differences. This initiative aims to help our Latter-day Saint community both understand and appreciate our neighbors of other faiths so that we can work together to accomplish God's purposes in the world. We hope this series will become standard reading in all of our communities throughout the world and will help us all to answer the lawyer's question: "And who is my neighbor?" (Luke 10:29).

Larry L. Eastland, PhD
Chair & President, John A. & Leah D. Widtsoe Foundation

Introduction

The Widtsoe Foundation launched two initiatives at about the same time. The first was to bring together eight prominent Christian scholars in writing and dialog about selected passages from the New Testament fundamental to their religious traditions, doctrinal understanding, practices, and where those understandings define their differences. This has been ongoing for the past five years. We have met twice a year in person.

The second was to commission and publish a series of books to help Latter-day Saints discover and appreciate the religions of their neighbors, and thus become better neighbors themselves. *Understanding Our Catholic Neighbors* was the first volume. *Understanding Our Jewish Neighbors* was the second. This third volume, *Understanding Our Evangelical Neighbors,* follows the same format as the first two. Each one is written primarily by a scholar of that religious tradition and co-written by a Latter-day Saint scholar so that it accurately describes that religion's theology and history on the one hand and is understandable to a Latter-day Saint reader on the other.

One of the joys of this combination of initiatives has been to become a part of the decades-long friendship between Dr. Robert Millet (emeritus Dean of Religious Education at BYU) and Dr. Richard Mouw (emeritus President of Fuller Theological Seminary). Both are devout in their own religious beliefs, yet wonderfully respectful of views and insights of the other.

This introduced all of us who have been involved in the New Testament Comparative Passages project to the concepts of "holy envy" and the three rules for understanding others' religions by the late Dean of the Harvard Divinity School, who was later elected as the Lutheran Bishop of Stockholm, Dr. Krister Stendahl.

This is beautifully described in Barbara Brown Taylor's book, *Holy Envy: Finding God in the Faith of Others:*

> Several years after his tenure as dean were over, Stendahl was elected the [Lutheran] Bishop of Stockholm and returned home to Sweden. He had only been in place about a year when he became aware of mounting opposition to a new Mormon temple opening in the summer of 1985. The antipathy was odd in some ways, since Sweden had a long history of welcoming religious strangers even then. It was predictable in other ways, since new religious buildings often cause more anxiety than new religious neighbors do—especially if their buildings are bigger and better looking than yours. The Stockholm temple was designed by Swedish architect John Sjostrom with a floor area of over 16,000 square feet and situated in a leafy suburb of the city.
>
> At a press conference prior to the dedication of the building, Stendahl aimed to diffuse tension by proposing three rules of religious understanding, which have by now made the rounds more often than any of his scholarly work on the apostle Paul. Here is the most common version of what he said:
>
> 1. When trying to understand another religion, you should ask the adherents of that religion and not its enemies.
> 2. Don't compare your best to their worst.
> 3. Leave room for holy envy.
>
> Stendahl's decision to stand with the Mormon minority in Stockholm was about more than his interest in the afterlife, however. "In the eyes of God, we are all minorities," he told a reporter shortly before his death in 2008. "That's a rude awakening for many Christians, who have never come to grips with the pluralism of the world."[1]

---

1. Barbara Brown Taylor, *Holy Envy: Finding God in the Faith of Others* (New York: Harper One, 2019), 64–67.

Holy envy means finding those things about another's religion that a person admires and appreciates—principles or practices that enlarge our appreciation for the goodness of God in all its varieties and ways of expressing joy in His presence in their lives.

These are the fundamental principles that have guided our *Understanding Our Neighbors* series. This volume, *Understanding Our Evangelical Neighbors,* is another chapter in the tapestry we call Christianity. We hope you enjoy it as much as we do.

Larry L. Eastland, PhD
Chair & President, John A. & Leah D. Widtsoe Foundation

SECTION 1

Evangelical Beliefs and Doctrines

1

Evangelicalism: A Brief Historical Account

By Dr. Richard J. Mouw

Evangelicalism is a Christian tradition that has encompassed people from many denominations and nations, that is, Evangelicalism is trans-denominational. The label "evangelical" comes from the Greek word *evangel*, which means "good news," or "gospel." Evangelicals identify themselves as people who want to be faithful to the central teachings of the Christian tradition.

At various points in Christian history movements have emerged by people who were convinced that many in the Christian community were departing from key Christian teachings. The sixteenth-century Protestant Reformation was an obvious case in point, when Martine Luther, John Calvin, and others led their followers to separate from the Roman Catholic Church. On a smaller scale, the "restorationist" movement that emerged soon after the American Revolution, of which the Latter-day Saints were a part, was a rejection of what were seen as departures in the Protestant churches from the vibrant faith of the New Testament period.

As Evangelicalism took shape as an American protest movement in the nineteenth century, it drew strongly on the "revivalist" spiritual energies that surrounded Joseph Smith in western New York state, but it began to focus more on theological concerns when evolutionary thought began to influence

Protestantism. Charles Darwin's *Origins of the Species* had appeared in England in 1859, and it quickly stirred up controversy both there and in the United States, focusing on how the theory of evolution related to matters of faith.

Darwinian thought reinforced what was already a growing emphasis on what came to be labeled "the doctrine of Progress." There was a general sense, especially in the intellectual community, that the human race was progressing to new stages in the capacities for moral, political, and religious development. This idea of progress began to take hold among many theologians, resulting in a re-thinking of many assumptions that had long influenced Christian thought. A growing trust, for example, in the gains of scientific research encouraged a re-examination—and in some cases an outright denial—of the more explicitly supernatural elements of traditional Christian belief. Many Protestant theologians began to play down the Bible's account of miracles.

For example, in one sermon, the topic was Jesus's feeding of five thousand people. A large group of people had gathered to hear Jesus speak, but the crowd became hungry and there was no food available for all. The disciples were concerned. All that was available, they told Jesus, were a few loaves and fishes that a little boy had offered to feed people—hardly enough for all of the crowd. Jesus told them not to worry. He received the small supply of food, and suddenly there was more than enough to feed everyone.

The story is told in the Gospels as a clear example of one of Jesus's miracles. But in the sermon that I read, the preacher said that in reality, the people had brought food for themselves to eat but kept it hidden because they did not want to share it with others. The boy's innocent gesture made them feel guilty about their selfishness, and when everyone started to share their food, there was plenty to go around. In other words, Jesus taught them to share. This way of construing what happened was clearly meant to downplay what the Bible teaches about the miraculous. The story of the feeding of the thousands is not about people being shamed into revealing that they had hidden their lunches. It is about the divine power of Jesus, the Son of God, to transform a small amount of food into a quantity that would feed a large crowd.

A sermon like this one signaled a change that was taking place in the Christian community. People were being taught about the power of moral improvement—encouraging individuals to draw on what was seen as our innate ability to act with sensitivity to the needs of others—rather than relying on the power of a Savior who entered into our human condition to change our hearts by atoning for our sins. This perspective took public shape in what came to be known as the Social Gospel, an approach promoted by theologically liberal Protestants that drew on Progress thinking in insisting that the Kingdom of God would greatly expand in the twentieth century through Christian peacemaking, programs of social justice, and other efforts to alleviate collective ills. This approach was aptly expressed in the name given to a modernist magazine established (and still in existence) in the final decade of the nineteenth century: *The Christian Century*—the coming century was going to bring major gains in the spread of the influence of the social teachings of Jesus. This is what is often referred to today as the rise of Mainline Protestantism.

While the liberal Protestants were anticipating decades of significant progress in spreading the influence of the social teachings of Jesus, Evangelical Christians were preparing for bad times to come. In the final decades of the nineteenth century they sponsored "Bible prophecy" conferences, focusing on "end times" scenarios about a coming period characterized by wars, natural disasters, and the deterioration of social bonds. When things finally get very bad, they taught, the true Christians will be "raptured" to heaven, and the final battle with the forces of evil will take place, prior to the return of Christ, with the establishment of His one-thousand-year reign as the—now to be acknowledged by the Jewish people—true Messiah of Israel.

* * * * *

During the first decades of the twentieth century, Evangelicals opposed the new modernistic trends, attempting to keep the major Protestant denominations and their theological schools within the boundaries of traditional orthodoxy. In their efforts, they emphasized what they insisted were the fundamentals of the Christian faith, the non-negotiable doctrines for preserving a genuinely Christian point of view. Human beings, they insisted, are sinners, desperately in need of salvation by divine grace; Jesus was birthed by a virgin, lived a sinless life, and offered Himself to the Father as a sacrifice for sin. He was raised from the dead and ascended to heaven. Presently on His divine throne, He will return someday as the glorious King. We learn all of this from the Bible, which is God's infallible Word to us.

The Christians who defended these teachings became known as the Fundamentalists, and they aggressively challenged those whom they saw as departing from the true faith. However, the Fundamentalists lost the battle for control and departed the Mainline Protestant church bodies. Some of them formed smaller denominations, but many of them established independent congregations, with names such as Bible Church or Gospel Fellowship.

Having basically been rejected from the established theological seminaries, the Fundamentalists established Bible institutes where practical training for Christian leaders was emphasized, thus replacing the more traditional subjects of graduate theological seminaries, such as systematic theology, church history, and biblical languages with courses focusing on practical Christian service.

The cultural pessimism associated with the strong interest on "end times" prophecy scenarios was now reinforced by an experience of cultural marginalization resulting from losing some key theological battles. Since American society was seen as destined to get worse and worse, there was little motivation to address social ills. The real mandates were evangelism and foreign missions. As the great evangelist Dwight L. Moody put it, since the ship of the large culture was sinking, the main task of true Christians was to urge drowning people to get into the lifeboats. The sea vessel imagery was also used specifically to counter the liberal programs of social improvement—efforts which were likened by the Fundamentalists to rearranging the deck chairs on the *Titanic*. The primary mandate for the Christian community was to help people avoid eternal damnation by preparing for a heavenly destiny.

* * * * *

In the post-World War II period, a younger generation who had been formed by Fundamentalism began to question what they saw as unfortunate traits within the Fundamentalist movement. A book by theologian Carl Henry, entitled *The Uneasy Conscience of Modern Fundamentalism*, came to serve as a kind of manifesto for this critique. While Henry remained convinced of the Fundamentalists' basic doctrinal convictions, he offered a bold critique of its excesses. Fundamentalism had downplayed—and even frequently ridiculed, he argued—the life of the mind. He called for a new kind of Christian scholarship that was faithful to biblical teachings while addressing the key intellectual challenges or our times, as well as issues of social concern. While the Fundamentalists were right in their insistence that the fulness of the Kingdom of God will only be revealed when Christ returns, Henry stressed that this does not excuse Christians from addressing matters of racial prejudice, poverty, and an over-reliance on military solutions to international tensions.

Since the labels "Fundamentalist" and "Evangelical" had often been used interchangeably, the movement that Henry and others came to lead was called "Neo-Evangelical"; gradually, though, simply "Evangelical" became the term of contrast to the older Fundamentalism. As mentioned earlier, Evangelicalism is not attached to a particular religious tradition but is trans-denominational. That is, it includes people who have in the past identified themselves as Baptist, Methodist, Presbyterian, Lutheran, Pentecostal, and so on but who share in certain core doctrine.

Carl Henry himself led the way in the causes he espoused. He was a founding member of the faculty at Fuller Theological Seminary, established in the same year that his book appeared. That school, along with Trinity Evangelical Divinity School, Gordon-Conwell Seminary, and others, including a network of Evangelical colleges and universities, became strong intellectual centers for the Evangelical movement. Wheaton College in Illinois, for example, came to be dubbed frequently as "the Harvard of Evangelicalism." In 1956 Henry became the editor of the new magazine *Christianity Today*, which continues to be a major evangelical voice in commenting on a broad agenda of cultural topics.

The Evangelicals disagreed among themselves about some traditional doctrinal matters, such as infant versus adult baptism, interpretations of what the Bible says about "the end times," the nature of ordination, and perspectives on how to understand the office and ordinances of church life. They tolerated their difference about such teachings, while maintaining a consensus on the key doctrines that had served as the basic convictions of the older Fundamentalism. In this regard, Billy Graham's ministry served as an expression of this emphasis on central gospel themes while tolerating disagreements on less central issues. For example, Graham welcomed the support for his evangelistic efforts from any church body that affirmed his calls for individuals to put their trust in Jesus Christ as Savior. Graham's espousal of "cooperative evangelism" was, however, firmly denounced by the continuing Fundamentalist faction.

* * * * *

While Carl Henry's leadership succeeded in promoting the life of the mind, as well as responsible journalistic efforts, the Evangelical community to which he gave leadership did not move quickly to social activism. Henry himself was a factor in this. During the 1960s, a decade marked by civil rights protests and vocal opposition to the Vietnam War, Henry argued that taking stands on social-political issues was a matter of individual Christian responsibility and not a topic for official church advocacy. Furthermore, he was clearly unsupportive of civil disobedience and disruptive displays of opposition to government policies. While he did frequently address societal concerns in his *Christianity Today* editorials, his views were not directed toward encouraging visible Evangelical activism in the public arena.

These patterns began to change at the end of the 1960s, when younger Evangelicals who had been in various protest movements during the previous decade—often to the dismay of Evangelical families and fellow church members—began to organize for a more activist approach. A key initiative in this regard was the establishment of *The Post-American* magazine by Jim Wallis and some of his fellow students at Trinity Evangelical Divinity School. Wallis explained the magazine's name by pointing out that some commentators were observing that the United States was moving into a "post-Christian America," but that it was time, Wallis argued, for Evangelicals to witness to a "post-American Christianity." (In 1975 the magazine changed its name to *Sojourners* and is still published.)

This new activism drew widespread public attention when a group of about forty Evangelicals gathered in a downtown Chicago YMCA in 1973 to issue a document called "The Chicago Declaration of Evangelical Social Concerns."[1] The Declaration began with this affirmation: "As evangelical Christians committed to the Lord Jesus Christ and the full authority of the Word of God, we affirm that God lays total claim upon the lives of his people. We cannot, therefore, separate our lives from the situation in which God has placed us in the United States and the world. We confess that we have not acknowledged the complete claim of God on our lives." The statement went on to call Evangelicals to work actively for justice and peacemaking.

Significantly, one of the organizers of this gathering was Carl Henry's son, Paul Henry, a political scientist who would soon be elected to Congress. He was joined by Ronald Sider, who made the Declaration the founding

---

1. "Chicago Declaration of Evangelical Social Concern," 1973, available at https://canvas.dartmouth.edu/courses/35388/files/5264567?module_item_id=329977.

document of Evangelicals for Social Action, which Sider would establish in the months after the Declaration appeared. The younger activists were joined in the Chicago meeting by several older evangelical leaders, including Carl Henry. While Henry had some qualms about a couple of the items in the Declaration, he clearly felt the need to put his stamp of approval on the younger generation's insistence on a more active engagement with issues in the public arena.

The Chicago gathering received considerable attention in the national media. Later the attention was expanded when Jimmy Carter, in campaigning for the presidency in 1976, identified himself as an Evangelical. *Newsweek* magazine then declared, in a cover story, that 1976 was "The Year of the Evangelical." In a few years, though, a very different sort of activism made its appearance when the New Religious Right became a political force in the 1980s. The most prominent of the movements in that brand of activism was the Moral Majority. And while that group no longer exists, the Religious Right is still a very visible voting block on the current political scene. Indeed, with the emergence of Donald Trump's national political role, many began complaining that the term "evangelical" has become so politicized that it is no longer adequately refers to a set of theological and spiritual convictions.

Others point out that the "politicizing" of Evangelicalism is primarily an American phenomenon and that millions around the world nurture Evangelical convictions without the influence of the "left" versus "right" debates that have come to dominate among their counterparts in the United States. Largely as a result of active Evangelical missionary activity during the past century and a half, the Christian churches have grown significantly in the southern hemisphere (Africa, Asia, and Latin America), and those Christian communities, which are predominantly Evangelical, carry on their witness without being in any way sidetracked by ideological conflict.

Even in North America, however, the Evangelicalism that is typically criticized for its confrontational political views is of the "white" variety. Many members of Black churches hold strongly Evangelical theological views but prefer to be called simply "Bible believers," while Hispanic and Asian ethnic groups similarly distance themselves from the "white" Evangelical churches. Some demographic studies have shown that younger Evangelicals across the board have become disillusioned with what they see as a mean-spirited older generation. The debates over the meaning and range of application of the "Evangelical" label continue. There is no question, however, that the ideas and attitudes that have been long associated with that label continue to be a major influence in the religious world.

2

General Overview of Evangelical Beliefs and Doctrine

By Dr. Richard J. Mouw

When a new generation of Evangelicals departed from the older Fundamentalist movement in the post-World War II years, they did not thereby abandon those doctrinal "fundamentals" that Fundamentalism had defended in the battles with liberal theology. They did reject some of the "Bible prophecy" excesses, as well as Fundamentalism's cultural pessimism and its legalistic patterns, but the basic convictions associated with the "fundamentals" were retained.

The beliefs that we single out as the basics of traditional Christianity have something to do, of course, with historical circumstances. When Protestantism emerged during the Reformation of the sixteenth century, for example, there was no real controversy between Catholics and Protestants over the full divinity of Jesus Christ. This did, however, become a key issue in the early twentieth-century disputes between Fundamentalists and their liberal counterparts, when the liberal desire to play down the more supernatural elements in the Bible led to a strong focus on Jesus as a gifted moral teacher.

For the Protestant Reformers, led by Martin Luther and John Calvin, the key issues in their arguments with the Catholic Church focused in a central way on questions regarding the nature of salvation. This can clearly be seen in Martin Luther's insistence on the doctrine of justification by faith. The more elaborate scheme for how Luther and others explained the issues regarding salvation was outlined in a set of five "solas" of the Reformation. The Latin world *sola* means "alone," and each of the five was an "alone" declaration: "scripture alone" (*sola scriptura*), "faith alone" (*sola fide*), "grace alone" (*sola gratia*), "Christ alone" (*sola Christus*), and "the glory to God alone" (*sola deo gloria*). Those five declarations also compose a good summary of the essentials of Evangelical teaching, and I will use them as my framework here for explaining those teachings. Again, these "solas" have to do primarily with an understanding of the nature of salvation, which is really what being Evangelical, a "gospel person," is all about.

Using these five declarations to explain the distinctives of Evangelicalism to Latter-day Saint friends is, as I see it, a good way of getting at the basics. When Robert Millet and I initiated our Mormon-Evangelical dialogue in 2000, we were eager to find a way to get at important topics without getting sidetracked by unproductive polemical exchanges. We agreed to steer clear, then, of some of the aspects of LDS thought and practice that had long been featured by "counter-cult" critics of Mormonism, particularly questions about the origins of the Book of Mormon.

We decided that the most fruitful line of discussion would be directed toward questions about how human beings "can get right with God." Why are we in need of redemption, and how do we enter into a proper relationship with the divine? As I will explain, the five Reformation "solas" give us a helpful framework for understanding Evangelical emphases on these matters—a framework that also allows helpful comparisons between Evangelical and Latter-day Saint convictions on issues of salvation.

Scripture Alone

In my late teens I read a book, *Fundamentalism and the Word of God*, by James Packer, a highly respected British theologian who was influential among the neo-Evangelical movement that had emerged after World War II. At that time I was beginning to think much about theology, and Packer's book was one of the first serious theological books I read. It clarified some important issues for me, as I was wrestling with how much I should hold onto from the Fundamentalism that was very much a part of my youth. Packer made it clear that while he himself was distancing himself from Fundamentalist excesses, he did want to hold on to the basic convictions that they had defended against the liberal theologians. Those convictions were, he insisted, at the heart of the Christian faith. They essentially composed the basic theology defended by the sixteenth century Protestant Reformers. Packer's perspective influenced me significantly as I set out on my personal theological journey, and it has continued to do so.

In his book, Packer focused primarily on the Bible's supreme authority over other claims to our absolute allegiance. In making his case, he gave special attention to two rival conceptions. The first of these was the authority of the church, which had been the key issue of dispute in the Reformation period. Much of Martin Luther's opposition to Catholicism had to do with what many Catholic theologians would agree were excesses in church practice. A well-known example was the practice of purchasing indulgences, where church members could pay certain amounts to a priest in exchange for a reduction in punishment in the afterlife for sins we commit in this life.

There were, however, deeper issues concerning where Christians were asked to put their ultimate trust. Catholic theology places a central emphasis on the historical development of church teaching, especially those doctrines formulated by the bishops, those that come from official declarations from the Pope, who is the bishop of Rome. In fact, the Catholic understanding of papal authority is itself a teaching that came to be accepted as the result of the historical development of church teaching. When Jesus met with His disciples, He said that He was giving Peter "the keys to the kingdom." Since Peter would later become the head of the church community in Rome, after which he would himself be crucified by Roman authorities, the Catholic church gradually developed the idea that the bishop of Rome should be the chief bishop of the church—a teaching that eventually became the doctrine of papal infallibility.

The Catholic Church certainly has always seen the Bible as God's authoritative revelation to human beings. But Catholic thought insists that the Bible should be understood *as interpreted by church authorities*. Furthermore, in addition to what the church determines to be the intended meaning of biblical revelation, church tradition—teachings such as papal infallibility, the immaculate conception of the Virgin Mary, and the like—are also to be accepted as revealed truths.

I bring this up not to argue here against Catholic teaching but to explain how the Evangelical understanding of the authority of the Bible was shaped by the debate with Catholicism at the time of the Reformation. The Reformers were convinced that Catholicism had departed from biblical teachings on key matters, and therefore they rejected the Roman church's claims of supreme authority. Thus when we are forced to choose between what we understand the Bible to say versus what church officials teach, we must submit to the Bible's authority.

The other major conflict that shaped Evangelical views about the Bible was the early twentieth-century opposition to liberal theology. Liberal Protestantism emphasized the need to rethink some longstanding theological ideas to conform to an intellectual climate that increasingly emphasized the importance of a "reasonable" understanding of the basic issues of life. And in this case that meant the continuing influence of Enlightenment thought, which emphasized human reason as the ultimate authority in deciding issues of truth, goodness, and beauty—not that early twentieth century liberal theology simply abandoned the idea of biblical revelation as a significant source of truth, but a strong effort was made to either discard or downplay those past teachings that did not sit well with people looking for a more "enlightened" perspective on the issues of life.

Let me offer a personal example. A local public radio station once invited me to engage in a dialogue with a self-identified "liberal theologian"—a scholar with whom I had engaged in friendly arguments on other occasions, to discuss why, after two thousand years, Jesus still continues to fascinate people (even people who do not claim any religious identity) as a spiritual and ethical teacher. When we were on the air, my dialogue partner led off by saying that Jesus must have been a powerfully impressive leader, since His immediate followers obviously could not simply accept the fact that He died, creating an enduring story about His rising from the dead. Obviously, he said, this can no longer be believed, but we do well to apply the key teachings of Jesus to some of the big challenges of present-day life.

I said that while I agreed with my friend's emphasis on the continuing relevance of Jesus's teachings, I believe that His claim to be the divine Savior, the eternal Son of God who entered into our sinful condition on our behalf, was confirmed by His miraculous resurrection. My friend cut me off at that point: "Oh, come on, Richard! You can't really believe that! People don't come back from the dead."

In a predictable Evangelical manner, I answered by quoting a Bible verse. The Apostle Paul, I pointed out, says in 1 Corinthians 15:14, that "if Christ be not risen, then is our preaching vain, and your faith is also vain." My dialogue partner's immediate response was: "Sure, Paul said that, but Paul was wrong. He was wrong about a lot of things: the status of women, sex, and many points of theology. I prefer to stick with the simple teachings of Jesus!"

We went on to have a good discussion of how best to understand those teachings of Jesus. But our exchange regarding the Resurrection gave the audience a clear picture of the theological divide between Evangelicals and more liberal Protestants. My friend was picking and choosing what in the Bible to believe, in the light of what is reasonable to the present day "enlightened" mind.

Now, when we Evangelicals insist that we accept the fulness of biblical teaching, we need to be clear about how we understand what God means to reveal to us in the Bible. Those of us who are called to give theological guidance to the Evangelical community realize that we have to guard against misuses of the idea that the Bible alone is our supreme authority. I will point, then, to a few examples of how we might foster some confusion when we say that the Bible is our supreme authority.

We need to be clear about the difference between what the Bible *says* and what it *teaches*. For example, in Isaiah 11:12, the prophet says that God will regather the scattered people of Judah "from the four corners of the earth." Does this mean that the earth is flat and has corners? No. The teaching here is that God will be faithful to His promises to His people, and the prophet uses a colloquialism to make this point. This distinction between what the Bible says and what it teaches applies also to other kinds of questions of biblical interpretation. The creation account in Genesis 1 says that on the third day God created fruit trees, and then on the fourth day He created the sun. Does this mean that the Bible requires us to believe that twenty-four hours after the first apple tree appeared on the earth the sun came into existence? As an Evangelical I do not believe that this is what we are being *taught* in Genesis. That story about creation is pressing upon us that everything that exists comes from the hand of an almighty God and not through a random process of chance.

Another related caution is about the *scope* of the Bible's authority. A common formula in Evangelicalism is that the Bible is our supreme authority in matters of faith and practice. It is our infallible guide to ultimate truths about God's purposes in the world and God's will for our lives. It is not a textbook of science or economics or political theory. It offers basic principles about how we are to conduct our lives in those and other areas, of course. But if we want to know how our bodies function, for example, we should take a course in human biology.

There is much more that could be said about what, for Evangelicals, the Bible is *not*. But it is more important to stress what the Bible *is*. The Bible is the supreme record and means of God's revelation to us about the most important issues relating to the human condition. The atheist French philosopher Albert Camus once wrote that the big challenge we have to face with utter honesty is "the desperate encounter between human inquiry and the silence of the universe." We believe—and here I refer to Evangelicals and Latter-day Saints alike—with all our hearts that he was wrong. There is a God and He has spoken. And we believe that we desperately need to hear and to heed what He has said to us. We find His message in the Bible.

Where Evangelicals and Latter-day Saints differ, of course, is whether the Bible is the *only* supremely authoritative book in which we receive God's supreme guidance. This is an important subject to keep discussing together. But it is important not to draw the lines of disagreement in the wrong place. Evangelicals believe that God speaks to us in other places. He reveals Himself to us in the beauties of nature. We learn more about God's will from gifted teachers. When we struggle with difficult challenges and decisions, we often sense the leading of God's Spirit in our deep places. For Evangelicals, however, all of these sources of truth must be tested by what God has revealed in his Word, the Bible. Whenever a claim to God's truth conflicts with the Bible's teachings, we must obey the biblical message. There are many legitimate authorities that we should take seriously, but when they contradict the clear teaching of the Bible, the Bible "trumps."

Having offered these explanations of Evangelicalism's "scripture alone" convictions, I need to add that we are not always consistent in our practice in this area. Evangelicals are guided in our understanding of biblical teaching by various historic Christian creeds and catechisms, and we rightly insist that these writings are subservient to the Bible—they are human documents meant to clarify what the Bible teaches us. Often, however, they take on a Bible-like authority of their own. The same holds for the theological writings of revered thinkers in the Christian tradition (Martin Luther, John Calvin, and John Wesley are obvious examples), as well as for respected present-day scholars, pastors, and organizational leaders. We need to glean whatever wisdom we can from those who have recognized gifts in discerning biblical truth. But we are not always aware of the ways that we elevate these teachings to a level that belongs to the Bible alone. Our critics do well to keep us honest on these matters. The Bible is, of course, an ancient book. But it is also the *Living* Word of God. In our theology, Word and Spirit go together. As we read and reflect upon the pages of the Bible, the Holy Spirit testifies to the truth of what we read and guides us in our understanding of what that truth means for our lives.

Faith Alone

"Therefore being justified by faith, we have peace with God through our Lord Jesus Christ" (Romans 5:1). That simple Bible verse led Martin Luther to initiate the events that resulted in the Reformation, and that emphasis on the need for faith in gaining salvation is a central emphasis of Evangelical thought and practice. It isn't enough, we insist, to be a member of a church—a mere "nominal Christianity" can't save us. Nor can people bring about their salvation by performing good works or by going through rituals to atone for specific sins. Being right with God requires something inside of us, something subjective—faith. This means personally trusting in Jesus Christ as Savior and Lord, relying on what He has accomplished on our behalf to bring about our salvation.

In understanding our Evangelical insistence that we are saved by faith alone, it is important to be clear about the "alone" part of it. This is an especially important topic for dialogue between Evangelicals and Latter-day Saints because the relationship of faith to good works is seen as a major issue between us. Evangelicals often accuse the Latter-day Saints of relying on good works for salvation, and the Latter-day Saints often feel that Evangelicals make salvation too easy by downplaying the importance of good works.

When we Evangelicals talk about faith alone, it would be helpful to immediately add "for salvation." Our works do not bring about our salvation. Indeed, the recognition that we cannot "earn" our salvation by performing certain acts, or by going through certain rituals, is essential to a proper understanding of what it means to be saved. Salvation happens when we accept in faith the gift of what God has done for us in Jesus.

This does not mean, however, that our good works are not important to our lives as Christians. We are called by God to do them, not as a means of gaining salvation but as a response in gratitude to the salvation that God brings about in our lives. Good works are essential to faithful Christian living.

Let's return to the verse in Romans that had such a profound influence on Martin Luther. We are, it says, "*justified* by faith." What is the nature of this justification, and why is it so important for the Evangelical understanding of the nature of the gospel? Our understanding of the meaning and means of salvation relies on what is technically referred to as *forensic* or *juridical* concepts. To put it more simply, salvation for us is understood in terms of a courtroom drama. Here is the scenario: We are each born into the sinful human race. As the old saying puts it, "In Adam's fall we sin all." Our fallen condition is one of guilt. We deserve condemnation from God, and there is nothing we can do to redeem ourselves. But salvation has been made possible by what God has done for us. This is by all reports Evangelicals' favorite Bible verse: "For God so loved the world that he gave his only begotten Son, that whosoever believeth in him should not perish, but have everlasting life" (John 3:16). Jesus, as the heaven-sent Savior, entered into our sinful condition and lived a life of full obedience to the will of the Father. As the sinless one, He went to the cross on our behalf, taking our sins upon Himself.

During our two decades of Mormon–Evangelical dialogue, one of our favorite spiritual expressions that we have experienced together is the singing of "How Great Thou Art," and this verse captures our shared conviction on this important teaching:

> And when I think that God His Son not sparing,
> Sent him to die, I scarce can take it in,
> That on a Cross, my burden gladly bearing.
> He bled and died to take away my sin.
> Then sings my soul, my Savior God to Thee:
> How Great thou art!

For Evangelicals, the courtroom-type explanation of what it meant for Jesus to take away our sin is essential. He took upon Himself our condemned status so that those who accept Him as our Savior are no longer condemned. Because of the cross, God declares us to be innocent. We have a technical theological term for this: we become beneficiaries of *the imputed righteousness* of Jesus. Having put our faith in Jesus, who suffered and died as our substitute, we are declared righteous by the Father. We are now "justified by faith."

Grace Alone

Since grace and faith are intimately related, I have already touched on the main issues regarding grace. A common way of putting it is that we "receive grace through faith." Having faith in Jesus, then, is our entry point into living as recipients of God's gracious gifts to us. The definition of grace is simple. Grace is *unmerited favor*. It is receiving what we do not deserve. "Gracious hospitality" occurs when people go beyond what we expected from them in making us feel welcome. When a car rental company allows a one-hour grace period in returning a car, it is giving us extra time that is not required by the terms of our contract.

The word "gratitude" shares a common root with "grace." When someone gives us something that we did not have a right to claim, the proper response is being thankful for the gift. In the Christian life, grace and gratitude go together. God gives us what we do not deserve, and we respond by offering our expressions—in word and deed—of deep thanks for what we have received.

We Evangelicals argue amongst ourselves about some of the aspects of grace. One major point of difference is how to understand the relationship between our individual decisions to receive, and our actual receiving of, God's gift of saving grace. One position, commonly identified as "Arminian," a viewpoint traced to the seventieth-century Dutch theologian Jacob Arminius, sees an individual's personal act of putting faith in Christ as initiating the process of that person's salvation, followed by God's graciously forgiving that person's sins. An opposing view, Calvinism, associated with the theology of John Calvin, sees God as planting the new life into the person's spiritual heart, with the experience of responding with faith in Christ being the individual becoming consciously aware of something that God has already done in that person's life.

That disagreement often leads to passionate theological debates, with the Arminians accusing the Calvinists of downplaying the significance of human free will and the Calvinists arguing that Arminianism treats the act of faith as a "work" that the sinful heart can produce prior to relying on divine "grace alone." The passion that goes into these debates can seem puzzling to outsiders. At the very least, though, they signal that Evangelicals place great importance on the teachings about God's grace.

Christ Alone

This emphasis on the uniqueness of Jesus Christ highlights the traditional Christian conviction about Jesus that the Apostle Peter proclaimed to the religious leaders in Jerusalem: "Neither is there salvation in any other: for there is none other name under heaven given among men, whereby we must be saved" (Acts 4:12). Evangelicals reject universalism, the view that all human beings will be saved. Active unbelief—a clear rejection of the claims of the gospel—is a matter of eternal significance. Evangelicals believe that hell is real.

The discussion of the *nature* of hell, however, is a topic of ongoing discussion. For some, the Bible's imagery of hell fire and the unending punishment of those who die without accepting Christ is to be taken seriously. Others find it enough to say that hell is eternal separation from God's good purposes. Many of us are attracted to C. S. Lewis's observation: in contrast to God's welcoming to heaven those who have regularly prayed to the Lord, "Thy will be done," He will in the end declare to those who have persistently opposed His purposes, "*Thy* will be done."[1]

There is much mystery surrounding the topic of our eternal destinies, and sometimes Evangelicals are careless in how we speak about such matters. I have heard it said, for example, that only those will be saved in the end who have made a conscious decision to accept Christ. It is doubtful, though, that any Evangelical would want to apply that to the death of a baby born to Christian parents. And, we can push it further: what about the deaths of children of *non*-Christian parents? And once we have opened up the discussion of those cases, can't we also allow some mystery regarding God's dealings with the millions upon millions of human beings who have never heard the gospel declared, beginning with all those who died before the Son of God entered into our sinful condition? This much is clear, though, on the basis of what the Bible clearly teaches: if a person is destined for heaven, it is only on the basis of the atoning work of Jesus Christ. Jesus alone saves—even as we can allow some mystery about how He takes hold of the lives of those whom He saves.

One of the areas where Latter-day Saints and Evangelicals seem to disagree has to do with what Jesus had to do to accomplish our redemption. Latter-day Saints have placed a strong emphasis on the agony of Jesus in the Garden of Gethsemane, and while Evangelicals do pay attention to that part of the story, we have seen the essential work of atonement as being accomplished by Jesus's sacrificial death on the cross of Calvary. My own impression is that we have often talked past each other on this subject. Evangelical theology does acknowledge that the atoning work of Jesus was a lifetime mission for Him. It isn't like He could simply come down from heaven for the event of the Crucifixion. It was necessary that He offer Himself on the cross as the sinless One who had experienced the suffering and temptations of our fallen human condition while perfectly obeying the will of the Father. The agony of Gethsemane was essential to this redemptive mission.

Nor do Latter-day Saints deny the necessity of the cross of Calvary for our salvation. The importance of the cross has been a special emphasis in general

---

1. C. S. Lewis, *The Great Divorce* (New York: Harper One, 1973), 75.

conference addresses by the senior leadership in recent years. Elder Jeffrey R. Holland's stirring address at the April 2009 conference, "None Were with Him," is an excellent case on point. It should be obvious that here are new opportunities for more constructive conversations between Latter-day Saints and Evangelicals, if we converse together with the eyes of faith focused on Calvary!

The Glory to God Alone

As I have been explaining Evangelical beliefs in terms of the *sola*—"alone"—declarations of the Protestant Reformation, the central focus has been on teachings relating to how a person gets right with God. The Bible alone is our supreme authority on topics of salvation. We are saved by faith alone. Salvation comes to us by grace alone. Christ alone is the true Savior. And the fifth *sola* offers an overall summary of the others: in our understanding the nature of our status as redeemed sinners, the ultimate glory belongs *to God alone*.

All of that has a clearly passive tone. We do not save ourselves; we are *saved*. Salvation is initiated by God. In faith, and by grace, we are *acted upon* by the Lord. But once that happens, there is a turn to the active. This too was emphasized by the Protestant Reformers, and it is an important theme in Evangelical thought and practice. We are saved to an active life of discipleship. Jesus's instruction to His original disciples extends to the Christian life today: "If ye love me, keep my commandments" (John 14:15).

In my Evangelical youth we sang a chorus, "Saved, saved to tell others of the Man from Galilee" (from the hymn "Saved to Tell Others, and My Sins Are Gone"). That song captured a key Evangelical emphasis: God wants us to speak to others about the salvation that can be found in Christ alone. There is much more, however, that God calls us to be and to do. Jesus's commandments range over all of life. The Westminster Catechism is an official Reformation-era creedal document adopted by the first generation of Presbyterians, but its first question-and-answer is often quoted beyond the Presbyterian world: "What is the chief end of Man? Man's chief end is to glorify God, and to enjoy Him forever." We were created by God to engage in patterns of living that glorify Him—in our family relations, our daily work, our stewardship, our teaching and learning, our play. All of life is to be lived to God's glory.

The way Evangelicals understand this emphasis on glorifying God in all of life has to be understood theologically against the background of our way of seeing the relationship of what happened in the human fall into sin. Since this is often a point of contention between Latter-day Saints and Evangelicals, it would be well to explain our perspective. God created Adam and Eve and placed them in the Garden to manage the affairs of the rest of creation in obedience to His will. When they disobeyed His command not to eat the fruit of the tree of the knowledge of good and evil, they rebelled against God and took upon themselves the sinful condition. God evicted them from the Garden, but He did not thereby abandon His creating purposes for human beings. Looking down on the fallen human race, He chose a people, the tribes of Israel, to show the rest of fallen humanity what it is like to live in obedience to His will. God revealed to Israel how He intended human beings to worship, to farm, to marry and form families, to engage in economic transactions, to work and play.

This same pattern carries over into the New Testament era. God saves us to live, individually and collectively, in conformity to His creating—and now redeeming—design for humankind. This Evangelical account of God's original purposes in creating humans, the fall into sin, and the plan of salvation emphasizes the themes we have been exploring here in our account of Evangelical theology. God created us to be agents of His will for the creation. We messed this up badly by our fall into sin, so much so that we are incapable of doing what is necessary to rescue ourselves. In sending the Savior to atone for our sins, God the Father was signaling that He had not given up on His commitment to the creation that He had, in the beginning, declared "good." The call for those who have put their trust in Jesus to become His disciples means that we are empowered to be agents of God's creating purposes. "Whether therefore ye eat, or drink, or whatsoever ye do, do all to the glory of God" (1 Corinthians 10:31).

The Doctrine of the Trinity

An important theological issue that must be made explicit is that Evangelicals are firmly committed to the doctrine of the Trinity. Since this is so central a doctrine for traditional Christian thought, and since Latter-day Saints reject the doctrine of the Trinity, many Evangelical scholars see this disagreement as posing an unbridgeable gap between our communities. I won't resolve the differences here, but I will explain the important role that our belief in the Trinity functions in our life and worship.

To begin with the obvious, the word "Trinity" does not appear anywhere in the Bible. Belief in a triune God is an *inference* from claims that we do find in the scriptures. Here are two of them, much quoted by Evangelicals. The first is what we label "The Great Commission," the mandate that the risen Jesus gave to His disciples before He ascended to heaven: "Go ye therefore, and teach all nations, baptizing them in the name of the Father, and of the Son, and of the Holy Ghost" (Matthew 28: 19). The other is the words of benediction pronounced at the conclusion of a worship service: "The grace of the Lord Jesus Christ, and the love of God, and the communion of the Holy Ghost, *be* with you all. Amen" (2 Corinthians 13:14). Our evangelistic mission is done in the name of the Trinity, and we ourselves are sent forth into our daily lives with the Trinity's blessing.

Throughout Christian church history theologians have debated specific points of doctrine about the nature of the Trinity, and these analyses have often gotten quite technical. What does it mean to say that each member of the Trinity is a distinct "person," while together they share the same "essence"? Or what does it mean to speak of three distinct Persons but to insist that they are one Being? If it is legitimate to say that the Son is "subordinate" to the Father, and that the Holy Ghost is in turn "sent" to bear witness to the Father and the Son, then is this only a matter of their "functions," or does it have to do with a difference in how they relate to the respective "Being" of each?

These discussions can seem maddeningly abstruse to the laity—and even to many theologians! But real theological issues show up in the larger community of believers that give rise to these explorations. Understandings of the Trinity diverge in two directions, each considered worrisome when they go too far. One of the worrisome directions leads to *modalism*. To use an everyday analogy, it is thinking of "Father," "Son," and "Holy Ghost" as different job descriptions. A person in the employ of a university can be a dean, a teacher, and a researcher—one person with three roles. In liberal Protestant circles there has been an effort in recent decades to eliminate—or at least to minimize—the use of gender language about God. The result is that the traditional Trinitarian benediction is replaced by offering the congregation this kind of parting formula: "May the blessing of God Almighty, the Creator, Redeemer, and Sustainer, abide with you as you go." This presents a picture of one God who has three titles.

The worrisome direction in the opposite direction is toward *tri-theism*, three separate persons sharing a divine essence. The analogy here would be three members of a basketball team's starting five: one is a center, one a forward, and one a guard; three individual players, but sharing the "essence" of being members of the Utah Jazz. Latter-day Saint understandings of "the members of the Godhead" is commonly thought of by Evangelicals as a version of tri-theism—although sometimes that view is labelled in harsher terms as polytheism.

My impression—shared by many who comment on Trinitarian debates within the traditional Christian community—is that those who reject each of the extremes actually do lean a bit, in stating what they see as a moderating position, in the direction of tri-theism, advocating what is often described as Social Trinitarianism. The reason for this is, I think, obvious: modalism does not do justice to the *three persons* aspect of Trinitarian thought. For example, consider the account of Jesus's baptism in Matthew 3. Jesus is in the water with John the Baptist, and the Holy Ghost is descending in the form of a dove. Then the Father declares from the heavens that Jesus is His "beloved Son." Clearly there are three divine persons present—three centers of consciousness.

What the scenario at the Jordan River does make clear to those of us who take the doctrine of the Trinity seriously is the *unity* of the Godhead. The late John Stott, one of beloved leaders in global Evangelicalism in the twentieth century, emphasized this point for understanding the work of Christ on the cross. There is a danger, Stott argued, that we see the Father as *over against* the Son at Calvary—a wrathful Father punishing His offspring in order to settle the accounts of our sinfulness. In the crucifixion, Stott said, the Father and the Son took the initiative *together* to save sinners. They were not subject and object, said Stott, but two subjects. It was the very same God, pouring out His wrath against sin, who also experienced the torment of the suffering that was necessary for our redemption. Calvary is all about the unity of the God who saves us. [2]

Typically, when theologians reach the limits of their technical treatises on the Trinity, they conclude by saying that the doctrine is enshrouded in mystery. It is important to arrive at that point. Ultimately our encounter with the divine Trinity is not something that we grasp intellectually. It is to bow in worship in the presence of eternal mysteries, as we sing in the hymn "Holy, Holy, Holy": "Holy, holy, holy! Merciful and mighty, God in three persons, blessed Trinity!"

---

2. John Stott, *The Cross of Christ* (Downders Grove, IL: InterVarsity Press, 1986), 156.

3

Beliefs in Common with Latter-day Saints

By Dr. Robert L. Millet

When we first began what was then called the Mormon–Evangelical Dialogue in May of 2000, all twelve of us (six Evangelical scholars and all six Latter-day Saint professors) wondered what we would discover. Would we basically disagree on every point of doctrine? Would we find that we had very little in common in terms of beliefs and practices? Or would we be surprised over areas of commonality? In preparation for our first meeting, all of us read a book that was essentially an introduction to The Church of Jesus Christ of Latter-day Saints as well as a book by beloved Evangelical theologian John Stott entitled *Basic Christianity*. In our first day of discussion, the BYU group responded to our friends' questions regarding many of our teachings and practices. There was no animosity, no debates, no contention—only earnest questions and answers. It was clear to us that in future gatherings we would have much to talk about as we discussed each doctrinal topic in greater depth.

On our second day, after singing a hymn and having a prayer together, Rich Mouw began our conversation by asking the Latter-day Saint contingent what questions we had after reading John Stott's introduction to Christianity. There was a rather uncomfortable silence. Each of the Latter-day Saints looked around and said something like the following to one another: "Come on. Isn't there something we strongly disagree with or some matter where we need clarification?" Nothing was said. Rich then inquired: "Has anyone read the book?" We all nodded in the affirmative that we had read and studied the text and enjoyed it very much. "And you have no questions?" Rich followed up. It was a fascinating moment. Finally one of the members of our group spoke up and said, "So far as I can tell, there's nothing here we would take issue with." We weren't quite sure what it all meant and wondered if our dialogue would end a day early.

Finally, one of the Latter-day Saints said, "Everything John Stott discussed in this little book is biblical, and we believe the Bible just like you do." A second person then added something significant. He said, essentially, that the reason we have no problem with the book is that Stott quoted the New Testament alone and did not rely upon any of the creedal statements about God and the gospel of Jesus Christ, matters with which *we do* take issue. When it came to discussing God or Christ or the Holy Spirit, Stott had confined himself basically to the four Gospels and a few passages from the epistles. That was an encouraging moment in those opening hours of a dialogue that would continue for over twenty years. We realized then and there that we would discover many doctrinal truths or Christian practices in which *we would* be in complete agreement.

In reflecting on what Dr. Mouw has said about the intellectual climate out of which Neo-Evangelicalism was born, it's important to note that Latter-day Saints passed through those same early decades of the twentieth century, when matters of faith were under attack in our own church. People in Utah also read Charles Darwin's *Origin of the Species*, and some came away with an altered perspective on human origins that seemed to be at odds with what latter-day scripture and modern prophets had taught—such matters as Adam and Eve, the Fall, the age of the earth, the flood in the days of Noah, and so on. A few members of the Brigham Young University faculty insisted on teaching their newly acquired worldview of the Bible to their students, and, in some cases, it cost them their jobs.

In the 1930s several Latter-day Saint professors entered graduate degree programs in biblical studies at the University of Chicago. What was the result? One senior leader of The Church of Jesus Christ of Latter-day Saints stated that after this collection of scholars had been immersed in literary-historical-critical studies of the Old and New Testaments (known until recent times as higher criticism) and liberal theology, all "returned but some never came home."[1] Another leader used this analogy: "Some of those who returned came back selling shoes for the wrong company!"[2] Members of the Church who have some awareness of twentieth-century Church history can thus identify with some of the challenges our Evangelical friends face.

Dr. Mouw has mentioned the "solas" of the Protestant Reformation regarding how salvation comes: *sola Christus* (Christ alone); *sola fide* (faith alone); *sola gratia* (grace alone); *sola scriptura* (scripture alone); and *sola deo gloria* (the glory to God alone). How do Latter-day Saints align with our Evangelical friends on these matters? There is absolutely no question but that salvation or eternal life is made available to the children of God by virtue of the atoning blood of Jesus Christ—and in no other way. As our Lord said, He is "the way, the truth, and the life" (John 14:6). It isn't just that Jesus points the way; *He is the way*. It isn't just that Jesus teaches us the truth; *He is the truth*. It isn't just that Jesus makes available to us life, the abundant life (John 10:10); *He is the Life*. The precious truth taught by the Apostle Peter to the leaders of the Jews, that "there is none other name under heaven given among men, whereby we must be saved" is echoed in the scriptures of the Restoration (see 2 Nephi 25:20; 31:20; Mosiah 3:17; 4:8; Doctrine and Covenants 18:23).

Of course it is by faith alone that we are saved. To have faith in Jesus Christ is to have total *trust* in Him, complete *confidence* in Him, and a ready *reliance* upon Him. Now, to be sure, true faith is always manifest in faithfulness, in dedicated discipleship, in obedience to God's commandments (see John 14:15; James 2:19–20). Our good works can never save us but rather manifest our love for and our gratitude to God for the unspeakable gift of His Son and His atoning sacrifice.

Early in the Book of Mormon, Lehi taught his son Jacob that "there is no flesh that can dwell in the presence of God, save it be through the merits, and mercy, and grace of the Holy Messiah" (2 Nephi 2:8). At the end of the Book of Mormon, Moroni spoke of those who had just entered into the Church of Jesus Christ, counseling them to be "watchful unto prayer, relying alone upon the merits of Christ, who was the author and the finisher of their faith" (Moroni 6:4).

---

1. Boyd K. Packer, *That All May Be Edified: Talks, Sermons and Commentary by Boyd K. Packer* (Salt Lake City: Bookcraft, 1982), 43.
2. Ellis Rasmussen, former Dean of Instruction at Brigham Young University, informal communication with the author.

Our Lord set the standard and established the pattern by which each of us should live and govern our lives. In the hours of Christ's suffering in the Garden of Gethsemane He uttered words that serve as timeless teachings. Matthew recorded the following: "O my Father, if it be possible, let this cup pass from me: nevertheless not as I will, but as thou wilt" (Matthew 26:39). In some ways, Mark's description of that sacred occasion is even more poignant: "Abba, Father, all things are possible unto thee; take away this cup from me: nevertheless not what I will, but what thou wilt" (Mark 14:36). In this passage our Lord uses the Aramaic word *Abba*, which is a term of closeness, deep endearment, what some New Testament scholars believe is essentially 'Daddy" or "Papa."

In the book of Moses (in the Pearl of Great Price) is found this account of the Savior's devotion to God the Father before Christ was ever born, and His willingness to be the chief Advocate for the Father's plan of salvation. God the Father sounded the question, "Whom shall I send?" to be my Son, to put the terms and conditions of my plan into effect? We are told that Jesus, who was God's beloved and chosen from the beginning, "said unto me—Father, thy will be done, and the glory be thine forever" (Moses 4:2). Then, at the close of the Messianic ministry, "Jesus, when he had cried again with a loud voice, saying, *Father, it is finished, thy will is done*, yielded up the ghost" (Joseph Smith Translation, Matthew 27:54; emphasis added). His entire life was devoted to carrying out the will and work of the Father.

I could go on and on, but this is sufficient to indicate that there are many matters in which Evangelicals and Latter-day Saints agree completely, and we should rejoice in those commonalities. While Latter-day Saints readily acknowledge that not all who learn of our doctrine will accept what we teach, it is very important to us that those not of our faith understand what we say and what we mean.

4

Areas Where Latter-day Saint Beliefs Differ

By Dr. Robert L. Millet

Roman Catholic Archbishop Fulton Sheen said: "There are not over a hundred people in the United States who hate the Roman Catholic Church; there are millions, however, who hate what they wrongly believe to be the Roman Catholic Church."[1] So very often we make comments, or, even more serious, we make judgments of other people or their faith based on deficient or faulty understanding on our part. In the beginning stages of our Latter-day Saint–Evangelical dialogue, there were many doctrinal concepts that we fully anticipated would prove to be major differences between us. After a more careful study and consideration of the various doctrinal topics, however, we came away from our conversation sensing that in some doctrinal matters we basically saw things the same way but had often used different words to explain the doctrine.

---

1. Scott and Kimberly Hahn, *Rome Sweet Home: Our Journey to Catholocism* (San Francisco: Ignatius Press, 1993), 1.

Sola Scriptura

It seems to me that to state that the Bible is the final word of God—more specifically, the final written word of God—is to claim more for the Bible and the prophets whose writings and sermons are contained within this sacred Book of books, than it claims for itself. We are nowhere given to understand that after the ascension of Jesus and the ministry and writings of first-century Apostles that revelations from Deity, which could eventually take the form of written scripture and thus be added to the canon, would cease. Latter-day Saints would therefore disagree emphatically with the following excerpt from the 1978 Chicago Statement on Biblical Inerrancy: "The New Testament canon is . . . now closed, inasmuch as no new apostolic witness to the historical Christ can now be borne. No new revelation (as distinct from Spirit-given understanding of existing revelation) will be given until Christ comes again."[2]

In a book entitled *The Formation of the Christian Biblical Canon* (1995), Lee M. McDonald, an evangelical scholar, posed some fascinating questions relative to the present closed canon of scripture:

- Was the Church correct in perceiving the need for a closed canon of scripture?
- Did or could the decision to close the canon possibly limit the Holy Spirit's future work within the Christian Church?
- If the Spirit's revelation was limited to the Bible we now have, is that necessarily a statement that the Spirit no longer can or will deliver significant, divine truth, except for that which is found between Genesis and Revelation? That's quite a bold position to take on the part of mortals.

I have a couple of related questions to pose alongside McDonald's:

- Who authorized the canon to be closed?
- Who decided that the Bible was and forevermore would be the final written word of God? Why would one suppose that the closing words of the Apocalypse represented the "end of the prophets"?

---

2. J. I. Packer and Thomas C. Odon, eds., *One Faith: The Evangelical Consensus* (Downers Grove, IL: InterVarsity Press, 2004), 42.

Latter-day Saints teach the same basic message that Jesus and Peter and Paul and John delivered to the unbelieving Jews of their day—that the heavens had once again been opened, that new light and knowledge had burst upon the earth, and that God had chosen to reveal Himself through the ministry and mediation of His Beloved Son and the teachings of His ordained Apostles. Latter-day Saints find themselves today in a hauntingly reminiscent position relative to the continuing and ongoing mind and will of God.

Frankly, as Dr. Mouw suggested, no branch of Christianity limits itself entirely to the biblical text alone in making doctrinal decisions and in applying biblical principles. In their search for answers, Roman Catholics turn to scripture, to church tradition, to the post-New Testament creeds, and to the magisterium or teaching office of the church. Protestants, particularly Evangelicals, turn to scripture, to the creeds, and to linguists and scripture scholars.

This seems, at least in my view, to be in violation of *sola scriptura*, the clarion call of the Reformation to rely solely upon scripture itself. In fact, in Protestantism there does not seem to be a final authority on scriptural interpretation when differences arise, which of course they do. The Bible is a magnificent tool in the hands of God, but it is too often used as a club or a weapon in the hands of men and women. For a long time now, the Bible has been used to settle disputes of every imaginable kind, even those that God and prophets may never have intended to settle.

I love the Bible. I treasure its teachings and delight in the spirit of worship that accompanies its prayerful study. It has been one of the joys of my life for the last forty years to teach the Bible, especially the New Testament. I feel very confident that I voice the feelings and perspectives of many millions of Latter-day Saints. My belief in additional scripture does not, however, detract from what I feel toward and learn from the Holy Bible, any more than the Saints of the first century who had only the Gospel of Mark would have revolted over the acceptance of the later Gospel of John. Studying the Bible lifts my spirits, lightens my burdens, enlightens my mind, and motivates me to strive for a life of holiness. Further, the same Spirit that opens my eyes and pricks my heart when I read Genesis or Psalms or Isaiah or the Gospel of John works upon my soul as I read the teachings of Nephi or Jacob or Abinadi or Alma, as well as the revelations given through Joseph Smith and his prophetic successors.

The Doctrine of the Trinity

There was one doctrine that the members of the Mormon–Evangelical dialogue felt confident would prove to be the greatest difference between us, one that we actually put on the shelf for several years before we engaged it. This was the doctrine of the Trinity or the Godhead—the Person of God, the nature of the oneness between the Father and the Son, and Their relationship with all of humanity. Almost all of traditional Christianity accepts the doctrine of the Trinity as Dr. Mouw explained it, based largely on the post-New Testament creedal statements; they interpret the nature of God through what is taught in those doctrinal formulations.

The creed that arose out of the Council at Nicaea set forth what is known as the *ontological oneness* of the Father and the Son (the word *ontology* has to do with *being*). The Father and the Son were said to be *homoousios*, a Greek word meaning "of one substance," or "of one essence." This means that while the Father, Son, and Holy Spirit are three distinct Persons, they are *one God, one Being*. This philosophical conclusion allowed the Christian Church to maintain a strict monotheism—a belief in one God—in response to the claim of Jews that Christians were polytheistic, believers in three Gods.

If the Christian theologians meant to convey in the creeds that the Father and Son are possessed of the same substance or same essence in that they are both possessed of the same divinity, the same divine nature, then Latter-day Saints would agree. Jesus Christ is the Son of God. He is God the Son. There was no facet of mortality that He was spared. There was no principle of the divine nature He did not possess. He was not 50 percent human and 50 percent God. He was fully human and fully divine.

I believe that New Testament teachings about the oneness of the Godhead are intended to be understood by the woman on the street and the man in the pew, not just by philosophers and theologians. In that light, consider scriptural passages that teach:

1. The will of the Son is somehow different from or subject to the will of the Father (see Mark 14:36; John 4:34; 5:30; 6:38–40).
2. The Father has power, knowledge, glory, and dominion that the Son does not have (see Matthew 27:46; Mark 13:32; Luke 18:18–19; 23:34; John 5:19–27, 37; 8:17–18; 11:41–42; 12:27–28; 14:28; 15:15; 1 Corinthians 11:3; Hebrews 1:1–4).

3. Christ's doctrine is not His but His Father's (John 7:16–17).

Over the years, I have asked traditional Christian scholars how they can read some of the above passages and still maintain that the Father and the Son are one being. They have often replied that when Jesus came to earth, He underwent a temporary subordination. But this idea is at odds with what the Apostle Paul taught to the Corinthian Saints. In writing of that great day in the future when Jesus "shall have delivered up the kingdom to God, even the Father," and "put down all rule and all authority and power" and conquered death, "*then shall the Son also himself be subject unto him* [God the Father] that put all things under him, that God may be all and all" (1 Corinthians 15:24-28; emphasis added).

Latter-day Saints could describe our belief in the oneness of the Godhead, based upon Book of Mormon and Doctrine and Covenants teachings, as follows: We believe there are three members of the Godhead—God the Father, His Son Jesus Christ, and the Holy Ghost. We believe that each of these members of the Godhead possesses all of the qualities and attributes of godliness in perfection. We believe that the unity, love, and commitment to the Father's plan of salvation that exists between these three divine Beings is of such magnitude that even modern scripture can speak appropriately of them as "one God" (2 Nephi 31:21; Alma 11:44; 3 Nephi 11:27, 36; Moroni 7:7; Doctrine and Covenants 20:28). This description could be called a variation of what Dr. Mouw referred to above as social trinitarianism."

In the October 2007 general conference, Elder Jeffrey R. Holland summarized the matter as follows: "We believe these three divine persons constituting a single Godhead are united in purpose, in manner, in testimony, in mission. We believe Them to be filled with the same godly sense of mercy and love, justice and grace, patience, forgiveness, and redemption. I think it is accurate to say we believe They are one in every significant and eternal aspect *except* believing Them to be three persons combined in one substance, a Trinitarian notion never set forth in the scriptures because it is not true."

5

Appreciation for Evangelical Beliefs

By Dr. Robert L. Millet

Professor Krister Stendahl served as dean of the Harvard Divinity School from 1968 to 1979. He also served as Lutheran Bishop of Stockholm during the late 1980s. During this time The Church of Jesus Christ of Latter-day Saints announced that a temple would be erected in Stockholm. As is often the case, there was much unrest and a great deal of anger expressed over a temple in that area, and many vicious and inaccurate articles appeared in the news media. Bishop Stendahl summoned a press conference and basically scolded the media and those who had reacted in such an un-Christian manner.

As part of his remarks, he made some very timely and deeply significant recommendations to the people of that area. He spoke of some principles of effective interfaith engagement that had guided him over the years: "Let the other define herself ('Don't think you know the other without listening'); compare equal to equal (not my positive qualities to the negative ones of the other); and find beauty in the other so as to develop 'holy envy.'"[1] As the Latter-day Saint–Evangelical dialogue went forward from May of 2000

---

1. Barbara Brown Taylor, *Holy Envy: Finding God in the Faith of Others* (New York: Harper One, 2020), 64–67.

to May of 2022, we tried to incorporate his advice and adapt them to our dialogue as follows:

1. If you really want to understand another person's faith, go to an active, participating, somewhat knowledgeable member of that faith and ask him or her your questions.
2. If you feel you must compare faiths, always compare their best with your best.
3. Always leave room for "holy envy."

"Holy Envy," therefore, represents those beliefs or practices of the other faith that we find attractive, meaningful, enriching, or spiritually uplifting. If we are willing to open our eyes to the goodness and sincerity of those who may believe or worship differently, we will come away more often from a conversation or interaction with feelings of love and respect; we begin to see them as God our Father and Jesus Christ sees them. In other words, we begin to see the truth, things as they are and as they will be (Doctrine and Covenants 93:24). We need not compromise one jot or one tittle of our conviction of the restored gospel when we choose to recognize and appreciate goodness, when we sense the truth, wherever it may be found. We begin more and more to prize highly the Fatherhood of God and the brother-and-sisterhood of earth's inhabitants.

Giving God All the Glory

First, I feel a holy envy for Evangelicals' emphasis on attributing glory to God consistently. So often in life when we have a moment or season of success, we informally or even unconsciously congratulate ourselves on our accomplishments, when in fact all that we do that matters, all that we do that will make a difference in this troubled world, will happen because our Father in Heaven inspired and empowered us to do what we could never do on our own.

Over the years, I have always felt uncomfortable when people offer compliments for a lesson or a sermon I have delivered. Those expressions have of course taken many forms. Some people say, "Good job." Others might remark, "Thanks for being with us. I learned a lot." I have generally been able to nod and thank them for their thank you. The toughest situations for me have been those where the individual tries to pay me a personal compliment, an overly gushy one, such as "You just gave an unbelievable presentation" or "You are such a wonderful teacher." For years I tripped over such compliments and tried to argue them out of it.

Several years ago, following a lecture at BYU Education Week, a woman came to the stand, shook my hand, and said, "You never cease to amaze me." I paused for a few seconds and then replied, "Thank you. The Lord was good to us today, wasn't He?" On other occasions I have responded with, "We were blessed tonight, weren't we? There was a wonderful outpouring of the Spirit." Such replies always made me feel better because I was doing my best to deflect any light or accolade away from me and back to the Father, the Son, or the Holy Spirit, the ones truly responsible for any spiritually rewarding experience.

The Beauty and Wonder of the Grace of God

Second, I am not sure that I would ever have come to understand the beauty and glory of the grace of God without my interactions and conversations with my beloved Evangelical associates. To be sure, the doctrine of grace is found throughout the Book of Mormon and the Doctrine and Covenants. It was, however, only after I had listened to, read, and reflected seriously on some prominent Evangelical teachers' and preachers' presentations on the merits, mercy, and grace of Christ that I began to see things with my eyes wide open. I was then able to go back to the writings of the Apostle Paul and to Restoration scripture and see the beauty and regularity of grace throughout scripture. It was everywhere.

Now, having acknowledged my indebtedness to an Evangelical perspective, I quickly add that I am not in complete harmony with all that Evangelicals teach on this doctrine. I have some reticence about the notion of imputed grace being only a legal fiction, that is, the idea that our worthiness is merely a divine pronouncement, a judicial decree, and not a statement about our actual pardon or forgiveness from sin. I believe that when the Lord forgives us, we are actually clean and pure. I quickly add, however, how much I appreciate the Evangelical church leaders and scholars whose teachings and writings pushed me to seek a deeper understanding and brought to me the peace and joy promised by the Savior and His apostles.

The Oneness and Three-ness of the Members of the Godhead

It may seem strange that I should express holy envy for a doctrine (the Trinity) that I denounced above. I do not believe in the doctrine of the Trinity as set forth in the creeds, but I am grateful for how those Christian church leaders and scholars through the generations focused on the *oneness* of the members of the Godhead. As a Latter-day Saint, I learned quickly and passionately to focus on the *three-ness* of the Father, Son, and Holy Spirit. Spending scores of hours reading papers and books on the Trinity through the last thirty-plus years has given me a deeper appreciation for how beautifully *one* the members of the Godhead are. As Elder Holland pointed out earlier, they are one in just about every way one can conceive, except for them as one being, one God.

Researching and reflecting on the doctrine of the Trinity has opened me to the teachings of the Eastern Christian Church, such as the Cappadocian Fathers. These remarkable men focused more on the three-ness of the members of the Godhead, and many of their teachings would today be described as social trinitarianism. As I now read the *Lectures on Faith*, particularly Lecture 5, I sense the depth of the teachings of the Prophet Joseph Smith and his associates who prepared and presented those lectures during the winter of 1834–35 in Kirtland. Better understanding how the Father, Son, and Holy Ghost are *one in mind* helps me to appreciate Paul's profound and comforting teaching to the Saints in Corinth that as we cultivate the gift and gifts of the Spirit, we begin to "have the mind of Christ" (1 Corinthians 2:16).

SECTION 2
Evangelical Religious Practices

6

General Overview of Evangelical Religious Practices

By Dr. Richard J. Mouw

An Individual Faith

Evangelicalism is often characterized as an individualistic faith, which is usually meant as a criticism. But for Evangelicals, a strong emphasis on the individual's relationship to God is a non-negotiable conviction. This emphasis is central for understanding the range and nature of Evangelical practices. I once had a conversation with a Catholic theologian during a public dialogue commemorating an anniversary of the Protestant Reformation. We had an interesting exchange about the individual character of salvation. In explaining the Evangelical view, I brought up the story of one of the thieves crucified next to Jesus. He asked the Savior to remember him when he entered into His Kingdom, and Jesus responded: "Verily I say unto thee, To day shalt thou be with me in paradise" (Luke 23: 43). I used that biblical example to make my Evangelical point. The interaction was between just the individual thief and Jesus—no church, no sacraments, no supportive community, no sermon explaining a point of theology. The thief simply recognized Jesus as Savior and asked the Lord for forgiveness. The Lord graciously granted his plea.

The Catholic theologian (he was a longtime friend, and we enjoyed our theological arguments) smiled and said, "Richard, you Evangelicals do like to get a lot of theological mileage out of isolated cases! You really can't base a whole theology on a brief conversation between a dying Savior and a dying thief." We need to look, he said, at what the Bible tells us about how things usually go in God's dealings with human beings. And we see that in the establishment of the church and its sacraments. The normal way to enter into salvation, he said, is to find forgiveness and healing in the community of believers.

I pushed back by telling him about a story I had recently heard from a man who testified about how he came to faith. He had come to a point in his life where he was increasingly successful in business. This involved considerable travel, and he had begun spending evenings in hotel bars. He had also engaged in promiscuous sex. He realized that his marriage was heading toward divorce. One evening, alone in a hotel room, he felt out of sorts, lonely for his family, and decided not to go to the bar. On an impulse he took the Gideon Bible out of a drawer and saw a page listing recommended Bible passages for persons experiencing certain moods: loneliness, fear, guilt, confusion, and so on. He began to read those passages and was overcome with a sense of being a sinner who needed to repent and to be forgiven. Somewhere he had learned that when people get religious they get down on their knees to pray, so he knelt at the side of his bed, weeping profusely, asking God for help. Soon he had a sense that his prayer was heard and that he was forgiven.

When he returned home, he told his wife about what happened and confessed his acts of unfaithfulness to her. They agreed to see a marriage counselor. After a while their family joined a church, and they started a new life together. I pointed out the obvious to my theologian friend—that in this case the actual salvation experience happened to the man alone in a hotel room. The life of the church eventually became important to him, but only after he had first entered into a personal relationship with God.

My Catholic friend was not persuaded by the story. "Do you really want to say," he asked, "that the church was not there at all? Who put the Bible in the room? Who wrote out the list of passages that a person should read? The church," he said, "had reached into that hotel room and drawn the man toward God. This was not just a 'me and Jesus' happening."

I acknowledged the legitimacy of the points he was making. But I was not willing to let go of the picture of an individual human being receiving salvation while kneeling by his bed in a hotel room, asking God for a new life. That was the beginning of a very personal relationship with God for the man who had sinned seriously, a relationship that eventually did require the nurturing life of the Christian community. So yes, it wasn't all about "me and Jesus," but that certainly was a necessary part of the picture.

Evangelicals call this type of experience being born again. The birthing image is important biblically. By God's grace, sinners are given new life. As the man in the hotel room came to faith, new possibilities opened up for his marriage and family. My friend Robert Millet regularly reminds Latter-day Saints in his writings of the wonderful promise from the Savior: "I am come that they might have life, and that they might have it more abundantly" (John 10:10). Evangelicals also look to that promise for the assurance of God's mercies.

Sacraments or Ordinances

In my friendly argument with my Catholic dialogue partner, we touched on an issue that also has significance for Evangelical–Latter-day Saint relationships: the role of sacraments in the life of the church. Actually, there is no consensus among Evangelicals on sacramental observances. Some of us practice infant baptism, while others hold exclusively to the baptism of adults. Some Evangelicals are drawn to Anglican-type eucharistic (sacrament of the Lord's Supper) celebrations, and others engage in less formal patterns of celebrating communion. Furthermore, we don't all agree on whether these elements of worship are rightly called sacraments or ordinances.

The vast majority of Evangelicals, however, do agree that baptism is not necessary for salvation. The exception here are groups within the Restorationist movement—Churches of Christ, for example—who do hold that baptism is essential for being a Christian. From what I have already said, it is not difficult to imagine what a typical Evangelical argument might be against the idea that baptism is required for salvation. The thief on the cross example would likely come up, as would conversion stories like my hotel room case. Most of us would certainly insist that if the convert had continued in his earthly life, his life as a follower of Jesus would have naturally led him to identify publicly with the community of disciples—including being baptized into that community and participating in the celebration of the

Lord's Supper with fellow believers. But these would count mainly as public affirmations of what had already happened in the salvation that had taken place when the individual had made a personal commitment to Christ.

Church Life

To emphasize the fundamental importance of a personal relationship with Christ is not to deny the importance of communal identity for the individual Christian. Evangelicals do emphasize the importance of church. In doing so, however, we generally take denominational identity less seriously than do Catholics and mainline Protestants. To be sure, the average Catholic or Methodist is often quite ignorant of what goes on in denominational affairs; for the most part, those matters are attended to by clergy and lay leadership. Clearly denominations influence the life of the local church. Many Evangelical congregations, however, are affiliated with no denomination at all, and even when a congregation does belong to a denomination— the Southern Baptist churches are an obvious example in this regard—much is made of the "local autonomy" of member congregations.

At the heart of the ministry of the local congregation is worship. Enthusiastic singing has traditionally been a significant feature of the worshiping life of Evangelicals. It is important to note that we share this practice with Latter-day Saints. When Emma Smith published the first Latter-day Saint hymnbook in 1835, the majority of her selections were much loved by Evangelicals. Evangelical hymnody has, however, changed somewhat in the past several decades with the introduction of "praise songs" into congregational worship. This mode of communal singing has been closely associated with the introduction of large screens in worship settings, where words of the hymns and pictures are projected. This has greatly decreased the use of hymnbooks, with the result that Evangelical worship has come to be characterized by raised arms during congregational singing. These changes have not occurred without some controversy, much of it generational in nature. Younger members show a distinct preference for contemporary praise music led by worship teams and musical ensembles including guitarists and drummers, while many of the older generation express regret about the loss of "the old hymns" with organ accompaniment.

The preaching of sermons has also been a key element in Evangelical worship, with the exposition of Bible passages being a standard pattern. Here too, though, changes have been occurring. Younger pastors have abandoned the formal attire of the past, often in favor of tee shirts and jeans, with sermon outlines and illustrations projected onto the screens. Weekly worship services are usually supplemented by Sunday School classes for children, frequently accompanied these days by classes for other age groups. In addition, weeknight activities are also sponsored, with frequent attention to diverse needs and interests: small groups who meet for Bible study and mutual spiritual support, sessions for teens, persons in recovery programs, singles, those recently divorced or widowed, and more.

While Evangelicals place a strong emphasis on Christian fellowship in local congregations, they also actively connect to others in the larger Evangelical community. The Evangelical movement has expended much energy in creating a network of parachurch ministries, organizations and programs that have no official church authorization but who foster important spiritual activities not easily sponsored by local congregations.

Reaching Young People

The parachurch network has been particularly prominent in evangelizing and disciplining young people. The Evangelical historian Joel Carpenter, in his study of the Fundamentalist movement in the 1930s and 1940s, observed that while more progressive Christians often looked down on the Fundamentalists as being uncultured, the Fundamentalist movement did possess their own version of cultural savvy. They may not have been given to visiting art galleries or attending opera performances, Carpenter argued, but they had significant insights into youth culture that resulted in important successes in ministering to young people.

Since outreach to young people has been a major focus in Evangelical parachurch ministries, it will help to look at two prominent examples in this area. In the early 1940s, Jim Rayburn, a student at a Presbyterian seminary, took on the assignment of finding an effective way to take the gospel to non-Christian high school students. He decided to establish a weekly club at a local school, and this was the beginning of the Young Life organization, which quickly grew into a national and then an international ministry. Young Life's approach is for Christian high schoolers and adult volunteer leaders to engage in relational evangelism with non-Christian students. Young Life formed a network of summer camps, where participants at the conclusion of a one-week program are encouraged to make a commitment to become a follower of Jesus. The organization presently has well over three hundred thousand clubs globally, served by almost seventy thousand volunteers across the organization.

Another prominent Evangelical ministry to teenagers is Youth for Christ, also founded in the early 1940s. This organization has emphasized large events: Saturday youth rallies, where high school campus leaders—often popular athletes and cheerleaders—give testimonies to their faith in Christ, accompanied by youth-oriented Christian music and talks by speakers who call for "decisions for Christ." Billy Graham started his career as an evangelist in the Youth for Christi organization. Like Young Life, this ministry also developed an extensive national and international reach.

My brief account here highlights the two differing overall approaches of these two youth ministries, with Young Life concentrating on more intimate club-type groups, and Youth for Christ sponsoring larger rally-type gatherings. But while the major emphases differ, the approaches are not exclusive—they simply order the priorities differently. This tells us something about Evangelicalism in general. The revivalism of the nineteenth century featured large and often enthusiastic gatherings. But it also stressed the importance of intimate fellowships. Both emphases have continued to characterize the Evangelical movement.

The parachurch network also promoted outreaches on college and university campuses. The best known of these are InterVarsity Christian Fellowship, Navigator, and Campus Crusade for Christ. InterVarsity is seen as the most intellectually oriented of the groups, promoting a Christian perspective on a variety of academic disciplines—facilitated in part by the organization's highly influential publishing arm, InterVarsity Press in Downers Grove, Illinois. The Navigator's ministry puts more of a stress on spiritual practices, forming prayer and Bible study groups. Campus Crusade, now known as CRU, is well known for its active evangelistic efforts. Its members are encouraged to inform non-Christians of "The Four Spiritual Laws":

Law 1: God loves you and offers a wonderful plan for your life.

Law 2: Man is sinful and separated from God. Therefore, he cannot know and experience God's love and plan for his life.

Law 3: Jesus Christ is God's only provision for man's sin. Through Him you can know and experience God's love and plan for your life.

Law 4: We must individually receive Jesus Christ as Savior and Lord. Then we can know and experience God's love and plan for our lives.

Many Evangelicals have criticized these laws as over-simplifying the claims of the gospel, especially when Campus Crusade members have participated in "beach evangelism" during the annual college spring breaks. In this setting, they distribute brochures that quote and explain these laws to their vacationing peers, hoping to engage them in conversations about spiritual matters. These efforts have often been effective means of evangelism.

Other Parachurch Groups

Over the years, Evangelicals have also created a variety of parachurch organizations that minister to Christians in specific vocations. The names give a good sense of their specific foci: Full Gospel Christian Business Fellowship, Christian Medical Society, Christian Legal Society, Fellowship of Christian Athletes, Promise Keepers (for men), Hollywood Prayer Network, Christian Farmers Federation, and Faith and Work. There is even a Christian fellowship for airline personnel that meets at several airport hubs for prayer and Bible study. The campus and vocational groups that I have described came into existence primarily for mutual Christian encouragement and motivation to bear witness to personal faith in daily work. Recently, though, there has been an expanded focus on how Christian faith informs the actual content of our working lives

A good case in point is the Fellowship of Christian Athletes. A Black Evangelical leader once told me that when he took on the assignment of serving as chaplain to a professional football team, he was expected mainly to offer "locker room prayers" before games and provide counseling regarding personal issues with individual athletes. The leader told me, however, that he soon began to see the need to address broader issues. Professional athletes need to receive expert counsel in financial planning. For many of them, marriage and family issues loom large, such as, what are the implications of a father of school age children being "traded" to a team in another city during the school year? How are athletes given guidance in experiencing sudden fame? What are the psychological and spiritual dynamics at work in a profession where winning games is a weekly preoccupation?

Parallel concerns emerge in other occupational contexts. How should Christian lawyers think, for example, about issues of truth in formulating their cases on behalf of their clients? How do leaders in food-providing industries understand the tension between promoting nutritional eating and catering to popular tastes? What does it mean for a Christian actor to take on the role of murderer or a promiscuous fraternity member? In taking on this broader agenda, these vocation-specific ministries have recognized that it is not enough simply to "witness to others" in our work places. It is also important to reflect upon the content of our work. How do we honor God's creating purposes for human beings in the actual conduct of our vocational callings?

This awareness of the larger purposes of the Christian life—acknowledging the Lordship of Christ in all areas of discipleship—has led to an increasing emphasis on the stewardship of creation and works of justice. These matters have expanded the ministries of organizations such as World Vision—originally established by Fundamentalists as a ministry to the poor, but now a major Evangelical non-governmental organization (NGO) with a global reach. Newer groups have concentrated on specific issues. The International Justice Mission has mobilized Evangelicals in strategies for combatting sexual trafficking. Evangelicals for Social Action has encouraged efforts for economic justice and peace-making. Other groups have taken on more conservative activist causes, such as right-to-life, "family values," and Creationist science.

Evangelical Influencers

A liberal Protestant educator once told me that she is impressed by the ways that becoming an Evangelical means "getting a lot of *stuff*." She said, "If you converted to my kind of Protestantism, you might get some kind of certificate to hang on your wall saying you're a member of our denomination, and maybe some sort of poster promoting environmentalism or anti-racism. But not much more. You folks, however, have your personal Bible to carry around, often with a fancy wrapper-cover embossed with a dove or lamb emblem. And you get bumper stickers, podcasts, books to read, TV preachers to watch, even a lot of new popular heroes!"

All of that is connected to the parachurch patterns I have discussed. While the local church has a significant influence on the spiritual development of Evangelicals, the parachurch network also has a major impact. In reality, the most important influences on the life and thought of Evangelicals come from persons who have no authorization by church bodies. For example,

Charles Colson, a well-known figure in President Richard Nixon's White House, was sent to prison for his involvement in the Watergate crimes. While serving his sentence, he had a transformative Christian conversion, as recounted in his best-selling autobiography, *Born Again*. After his release from prison, he became active in the Evangelical movement. His prison experience motivated him to form Prison Fellowship, a ministry focusing on both evangelism and prison reform.

Colson rather quickly became an Evangelical superstar, writing and speaking about being guided in our lives by a Christian worldview. He attained this authoritative status within the Evangelical community, even though he had no theological education, nor did he have any formal office in any church body. The vast majority of the many Christians who revered him as an important Evangelical leader would not have been able to tell you what church he belonged to. (He was a member of a local Presbyterian congregation.) Colson's path to Evangelical stardom obviously had much to do with his previous White House role. His was a "celebrity conversion."

Another example is about a transition to fame from a quite ordinary life context. Ann Voskamp is a farmer's wife and a mother of seven children who lives in rural Ontario, Canada. Her 2011 book, *One Thousand Gifts: A Dare to Live Fully Right Where You Are* is one of her four *New York Times* best-sellers. Her blog posts are widely read among Evangelical women, and her Facebook page has more than half a million followers. Voskamp's Evangelical reflections, illustrated in daily reports about rural family life, center on the importance of having a profound sense of gratitude to God in the midst of the blessings and challenges of ordinary life.

How do individuals like Colson and Voskamp attract such large Evangelical followings? The question might not seem too difficult to answer in our age of social media. A person "likes" something or someone on TikTok or Instagram or Facebook, a commendation that can be seen by their friends who then pass it along to their contacts, resulting in thousands of people seeing the post. These days the folks who gain star status in this manner are known as influencers—an accolade that is closely identified with marketing strategies. Evangelicals have learned to use these means of communicating as effectively as others. But Colson's emergence as an Evangelical leader preceded the emergence of web-based social media, and Ann Voskamp began attracting readers to her blogs before TikTok-type systems introduced high-speed networking.

How these persons become Evangelical stars, then, cannot be explained simply in terms of contemporary marketing patterns. The answer is closely related to the web-based influencer phenomenon. People who are influenced by Instagram posts and TikTok videos *want* to be influenced. They are *looking* for ideas, products, and personalities that can add meaning or pleasure to their lives. Charles Colson came to be revered by Evangelicals because he spoke to their spiritual needs. They wanted reassurance regarding the power of the gospel to change lives, and Colson was a classic illustration. Similarly, the thousands of women who faithfully read Ann Voskamp's writings are looking for spiritual inspiration and encouragement in their daily challenges and preoccupations.

The personalities and programs accessible though the network of parachurch associations speak to interests and concerns that go beyond what local congregations can offer. To say that the Evangelical movement has developed effective marketing strategies is certainly true, but there's more to it than that. What is being "marketed" addresses spiritual yearnings that reside in the deep places of the human spirit.

Rules of Behavior

Evangelicals and Latter-day Saints share common patterns in the ways that our communities prescribe and discourage specific personal behaviors. Even though our respective rules are shaped by different histories, we have some of the same prohibitions. The practice of rather strict monitoring of personal behaviors was especially prevalent in the older Fundamentalist movement, as could be seen in the behaviors forbidden at the Bible colleges and institutes: no tobacco, alcohol, theater attendance, premarital sexual intimacy, dancing, and, even in many Fundamentalist schools, no card-playing or billiards. Those negative rules were relaxed considerably in the "neo-Evangelicalism" that emerged in the post-World War II era, although Evangelical colleges and universities still retain a few of these prohibitions.

A key factor that has been at work in this focus on personal behaviors has been a desire to avoid worldliness. Evangelicals look to, among other biblical passages, Romans 12:2 in this regard: "And be not conformed to this world: but be ye transformed by the renewing of your mind, that ye may prove what is that good, and acceptable, and perfect, will of God." The world in this sense is the fallen patterns of human life. Christians are called to bear witness to redeemed patterns of behavior.

We find the same warning against conformity to the world elsewhere in the New Testament: "Love not the world, neither the things that are in the world. If any man love the world, the love of the Father is not in him" (1 John 2:15). The way the Apostle John puts it here, however, raises an interesting question. When he tells us in this passage that when we love the world we are contradicting the will of the Father, isn't this in conflict with what John the Beloved says in the much-quoted passage from his Gospel? Jesus said: "For God *so loved the world*, that He gave His only begotten Son" (John 3:16; emphasis added).

There really is no genuine conflict in this. The word "world" in the Bible has at least three meanings. It refers, as we have already seen, to human fallenness—the bad patterns and lifestyles that Christians are called to avoid. It can also have a simple physical meaning: the world as the geographic expanse of reality, as when the risen Jesus tells His disciples to "go ye into all the world, and preach the gospel to every creature" (Mark 16:15). But there is also "world" in the sense of the good creation. In John 3:16 the English word "world" is a translation for the Greek term *kosmos*—which is the universal *order* of reality. And in the next verse John writes that in sending the Son into the world, it was not God's intention "to condemn the world; but that the world through him might be saved" (John 3:17).

God still loves all that He created, and while Jesus certainly entered into the world to save sinners, He also came to reclaim all of that which God originally called into being: "And God saw everything that he had made, and, behold, it was very good" (Genesis 1:31). This awareness of God's continuing love for the created order has inspired efforts in recent years, especially among younger Evangelicals, to work for "creation care," with an increasing concern about climate change, recycling, and the stewardship of natural resources.

Political Evangelicalism

It would not make sense to attempt to explain Evangelicalism to Latter-day Saints without discussing how many people now insist that the label "Evangelical" has outlived its usefulness. The label, they say, has come to have such strong political connotations that it no longer communicates what it has stood for in the past. Many who have gladly owned the label for much of their lives have been "resigning" from the movement.

This is not the place to go into the details of these matters, nor to advocate for my own views on the subject—except to say that I am not ready to abandon the label. On all sides, however, people agree that a key factor in proposing that the word "Evangelical" be dropped is the way many Evangelicals in recent years have actively pursued a "culture wars" agenda. In two successive presidential elections, more than 80 percent of self-identified Evangelicals voted for Donald Trump, giving enthusiastic support for his views on immigration policy, attitudes toward Muslims, restoring America's "greatness" in international relations, and so on.

To be sure, none of this suddenly emerged with the appearance of Donald Trump on the national political scene. Already in the early 1970s, as we have seen, younger Evangelicals called for a more active political engagement—albeit on issues that differ significantly from those being espoused by "political Evangelicals" in the contemporary context. Then in the 1980s Jerry Falwell led the Moral Majority, giving visibility to what came to be known as the New Christian Right. The more recent manifestation of Rightist political activism is continuous with those developments.

What was happening in this change earlier in the twentieth century, when Evangelicals were seen as "a-political"? When I was growing up in an Evangelical home, my parents and others in our network of family and friends consistently voted Republican. If they ever heard any political advocacy in church it was a few words of encouragement to be good citizens. No one in this extended network was particularly angry about issues of public life. I remember my father saying that he had even voted once for Franklin Roosevelt because "he did some good things."

The Cold War period raised some concerns about the influence of communism, but in my world that never took the form of a passionate activism. The real changes, as I read the history, came with the sexual revolution of the 1960s. The combination of new forms of birth control, the legalization of abortion, and the popularity in the larger culture of *Playboy*-like promiscuity signaled a dramatic change in public morality

To be sure, the civil rights movement and anti-war demonstrations also contributed to Evangelical worries about what was happening in the larger culture. My own political views on these matters caused considerable consternation in my family. But the more basic mood was one of a deep anxiety about social trends. Sex education in the schools caused parents to worry about how their children's values were influenced. Reports about school lessons featuring "Heather has two mommies" and a more aggressive teaching of evolutionary thought inspired the establishing of new "Christian schools" and eventually to the spread of homeschooling.

The New Christian Right came into being to reclaim what were seen as traditional American values. And the idea that Evangelicals could work with others with whom they shared moral convictions—Catholics and Latter-day Saints in particular—helped to encourage a shift from Evangelicals seeing themselves as a marginalized minority to a sense of being a movement that could join in efforts of social change that might actually accomplish something positive.

The issues at stake here will be familiar to Latter-day Saints. The Saints have gone through several shifts in their own understanding of their place in American society since Joseph Smith established the Church in 1830. When we see ourselves as a beleaguered minority, we develop spiritual and theological resources that concentrate on *survival* as a movement. Those ways of understanding ourselves change significantly when we cultivate some optimism about our ability to work for societal change.

Fundamentalism was very much a "survival" form of Christianity. Bible prophecy themes promoted the idea that things would inevitably deteriorate in the larger culture, which meant that the primary Christian tasks were to cultivate a strong sense of in-group identity while encouraging people to get ready for heaven. The self-understanding of Evangelicals is very different these days, due in large part to electoral victories.

The danger in both of our communities is that we will not see these changes as requiring careful theological reflection on what it means to promote faithfully the cause of the gospel as understood within our respective faith traditions. Furthermore, all of this is complicated by the potential for growing generational divides. Scholars and journalists are giving attention to a younger generation that does not share past allegiances to church identities and practices. The "Nones"—young people who claim no religious affiliation—are not against religion as such, but they do rebel against institutional authority and faith-based behavioral codes—as evidenced in the oft-quoted comment that "I may not be religious, but I do see myself as a *spiritual* person." The importance of thinking carefully about these matters is not only significant for understanding our roles as citizens but also for effective inter-generational conversation.

Closely tied to gaining a proper theological understanding of our role as citizens is the nurturing of a spirituality that informs our public engagement. What are the Christian virtues that should characterize our presence in American political life? A Muslim leader from Indonesia reinforced the importance of this concern for me when he described the challenge that he experiences with the younger Muslims in his country. "They go in one of two different directions," he said. "Some of them are attracted to a radical version of Islam because it promises that we can do things that can quickly bring about the right kinds of changes. The others are not up to that kind of commitment and simply give up and keep their faith private. In each option, what is missing is the patience that is necessary to work at good things for the long haul!"

The Muslim leader's description has its parallel in Evangelicalism. Being a follower of Jesus requires a patience for the long haul. Only when the Savior returns will the decisive victory over sinfulness happen. But that does not mean that we should sit back and wait passively for Jesus to come again. In the meantime, we can do what is possible to work for good causes, which requires patience. And it requires other things, as well: respect for those with whom we disagree; a loving spirit; a willingness to bear witness to the grounds for our hope in the future that the Lord has promised to us. All of this requires what we Evangelicals have come to describe as *spiritual formation*. Our lives as believers include our engagement alongside of others in the public square. In our roles as citizens, too, we must be formed by sustained practices of prayer, the study of revealed truth, and meditating on the Person and work of Christ, who is the Lord of all of life.

7

Practices in Common with Latter-day Saints

By Dr. Robert L. Millet

An Individual Faith

Active and involved members of The Church of Jesus Christ of Latter-day Saints would readily agree that salvation does not come to groups; salvation, which is eternal life (see Doctrine and Covenants 6:13; 14:7), is an individual matter. People do not as a group gain a testimony that Jesus is the Christ, nor do we make group covenants, nor are groups of individuals baptized or confirmed. Just as Jesus ministered one by one (see 3 Nephi 11:15; 17:25; 18:36), healed the sick, caused the blind to see and the deaf to hear, and even raised people from the dead, so we "come unto Christ" and are perfected in Him (Moroni 10:32) one person at a time. Nor can an individual patron go into the temple and be endowed for and in behalf of hosts of ancestors in the same endowment session. We receive the gospel, make covenants, and participate in the appropriate ordinances on our own, one by one.

Now, we believe that the man in the hotel room that Dr. Mouw referred to above did indeed, like the prodigal son, "come to himself" (Luke 15:17).

He acknowledged how he had betrayed his wife and children and sinned against God, and he began the long and painful trek back to his waiting and ever-loving Father in heaven. After having exercised faith in Jesus Christ, been baptized, and received the gift of the Holy Ghost, the penitent person is justified—forgiven of sin, pardoned, exonerated, and brought back into a proper relationship with Deity. He may have, and in most cases certainly would have been, assisted on his way to the baptismal service, but the decision to follow and seek to emulate Jesus Christ was a promise he alone could make.

Christianity entails more than prayer, fasting, and searching the scriptures—more than an individual effort to live the principles of the gospel of Jesus Christ. As vital as personal devotion and individual effort are, Christianity is fully lived out only *in community.* The Greek term used to describe those who congregate in the name of Jesus Christ refers to those who are or have been "called out" and are "elect." Without the Church, one cannot receive the requisite ordinances of salvation; cannot develop those Christlike qualities and attributes that come only through association and affiliation with other men and women, boys and girls, who are striving for basically the same things; cannot participate in the ongoing service and "organized sacrifice" that can come only through working with others. Without the Church and Church affiliation and involvement, one simply cannot cultivate the gospel light that emanates freely and enticingly from striving and stretching members of the Church.

The Apostle Paul indicates in his letter to the Ephesian Saints that the various officers and callings of the Church were established for "the perfecting of the saints, for the work of the ministry, for the edifying of the body of Christ: till we all come in the unity of the faith, and of the knowledge of the Son of God, unto a perfect [person], unto the measure of the stature of the fulness of Christ" (Ephesians 4:11–13). When the gospel of Jesus Christ, as contained in holy scripture, is taught in its plainness and simplicity in our church meetings, unity of the faith results. The followers of the Savior thereby speak the same language and teach the same eternal truths. The members "are no longer to be children, tossed about the waves and whirled around by every fresh gust of teaching, dupes of cunning rogues and their deceitful schemes. Rather we are to maintain the truth in a spirit of love; so shall we fully grow up unto Christ" (Ephesians 4:11–15; Revised English Bible).

In a general conference of the Church, President Dallin H. Oaks, a modern Apostle and senior officer of the Church, spoke of the necessity of a church organization: "Attendance and activity in a church," he pointed out, "help us become better people and better influences on the lives of others. In church we are taught how to apply religious principles. We learn from one another. A persuasive example is more powerful than a sermon. We are strengthened by associating with others of like minds. In church attendance and participation, our hearts are, as the Bible says, 'knit together in love' (Colossians 2:2)."[1]

Reaching Young People

Our day is not like any time I have ever known, when millions upon millions, young and old, have walked away from organized religion, declaring themselves, as Dr. Mouw mentioned above, "spiritual but not religious." Leaders within The Church of Jesus Christ of Latter-day Saints are constantly reminding members of the faith of the importance of reaching out, touching, demonstrating Christlike love, and emphasizing the relevance of the gospel of Jesus Christ and the importance of His Church to young people. They are the hope of Israel, Zion's Army, leaders of the future. They are the ones who will preside over the Relief Society (the Church's organization for women), the Primary (the Church's organization for young children), the Sunday School (members twelve and older), and the priesthood quorums (men, both young and old).

The Church is making many attempts to hold on to our young people and fortify them against false doctrine and evil practices. First, high school-aged members are encouraged to attend weekday religious education called seminary. Here they meet and study the Bible, scriptures of the Restoration and the history of The Church of Jesus Christ of Latter-day Saints from Joseph Smith to the present, under the direction of a called or appointed teacher.

College-aged students can apply to attend Brigham Young University, a Church-owned institution where they may pursue their education in an atmosphere of faith. Currently there are 33,000 full-time students. The flagship institution is Brigham Young University in Provo, Utah, but there are

---

1. Dallin H. Oaks, "The Need for a Church," *Liahona*, November 2021, 24.

also BYU campuses in Rexburg, Idaho and Laie, Hawaii. In these three universities, religion courses are part of the students' overall curriculum. Thus along with their classes in English, physics, calculus, and biology, students enroll in religion courses. Students are required to take fourteen credit hours of religion in order to graduate. In a sense, each student leaves the university with a minor in religion.

Students who do not choose to attend a Church-sponsored school but enroll in a university or local college may attend the Institute of Religion, a weekday religious education program held adjacent to a university or college. In addition to scripture courses, university students can attend such institute classes as Christian History, World Religions, The Parables of Jesus, Missionary Preparation, Women and the Scriptures, Christ and the Everlasting Gospel, The Gospel and the Productive Life, Scripture Study and the Power of the Word, Dating and Courtship, and the Eternal Family. Institute buildings provide a restful atmosphere where students may study and socialize.

Second, the Church's missionary program is perhaps the strongest influence on young people of anything within the Church. Young men from ages eighteen to twenty-six and young women from ages nineteen to twenty-six may be called to serve as a full-time missionary for a period of eighteen to twenty-four months. They are called to serve by the President of the Church and are assigned somewhere within the United States or in scores of countries throughout the world. All missionaries receive their preparation for service in Missionary Training Centers (MTC), located throughout the world, where they learn how to present the restored gospel to the people of the world. Those who have been called to serve in foreign-speaking missions attend the MTC for a longer period of time so that they can learn the fundamentals of the foreign language they will soon be speaking, as well as important cultural factors within the country in which they will labor.

A full-time mission is perhaps the most powerful and effective leadership program we have in the Church. These young people return with a depth and a breadth and an elevated perspective on the purpose of life that will serve as a spiritual foundation for the rest of their lives. They also come to love and admire the people in the various states or nations and feel a deep kinship with them. Many young people attending Brigham Young University in Provo, Utah, return from their missions and become employed at the MTC to train prospective missionaries.

In addition, the Church has created single adult wards (congregations), where the members may associate with unmarried persons their own age. In some cases, single adult wards result in strong friendships and support systems, and in many cases, marriage.

Influence in Society

Because Latter-day Saints represent a small percentage of the world's population (almost 17 million in 2021), our overall influence would not be anywhere near the influence of Evangelicals throughout the world (in 2016, 619 million, one out of every four Christians). And yet the Latter-day Saints have had, in some ways, a disproportionate influence in society, given our relatively small numbers.

Prominent Latter-day Saint political figures include Ezra Taft Benson, a member of the Quorum of the Twelve Apostles and two-term Secretary of Agriculture under President Dwight D. Eisenhower; George Romney, governor of Michigan; Mitt Romney, governor of Massachusetts and Presidential candidate; Harry Reid and Orrin Hatch, members of the Senate; Glenn Beck, political commentator.

Business leaders include Gary Crittenden, former CFO of Sears Roebuck; Kevin Rollins, former CEO of Dell, Inc.; Nolan Archibald, CEO of Black and Decker; Alan Ashton, co-founder of Word Perfect Corp.; J. Willard Marriott, founder of the Marriott Hotel chains; David Neeleman, founder of Jet Blue Airlines; K. Whitmore, former CEO of Eastman Kodak; and Stephen R. Covey, co-founder of Franklin-Covey Corporation and author of the best-selling book *The 7 Habits of Highly Effective People.*

Rules of Behavior

Members of The Church of Jesus Christ of Latter-day Saints are taught the importance of living the Ten Commandments, being obedient to the teachings of Jesus Christ, and in general observing what has come to be known as the Judeo-Christian ethic. The leaders of the Church have, through the generations, repeatedly charged the people to be *in the world* but *not of the world* (see John 17:14–16). Latter-day Saints believe there are absolute truths and absolute values, principles and standards of behavior that cannot be overturned by societal consensus or even by legislation. The whole world may conclude that there is no God, but God exists nevertheless.

Every human being on earth may decide that good is evil and evil is good (see Isaiah 5:20), but God's laws of behavior, as set forth in scripture and the words of prophets, do not change. For example, the Church has one standard of moral behavior: the only type of sexual expression that is approved of God is between one man and one woman who have been legally and lawfully wedded.

In February of 1833, the Lord revealed to Joseph Smith a law of health known as the Word of Wisdom. It encouraged the eating of wholesome grains and cautioned against alcohol, tobacco, coffee, and tea, and even to be moderate in the eating of meat. The Saints' observance of the Word of Wisdom has resulted in a people who are among the healthiest throughout the world. This law was not, however, just about producing healthy physical bodies, as important as that is. Notice the promises to those who abide by these standards: "And all saints who remember to keep and do these sayings, walking in obedience to the commandments, shall receive health in their navel and marrow to their bones." There is the stated benefit to the body. The revelation continues by speaking of the benefits to the soul: "And *shall find wisdom and great treasures of knowledge, even hidden treasures*; and shall run and not be weary, and shall walk and not faint. And I, the Lord, give unto them a promise, that *the destroying angel shall pass by them, as the children of Israel, and not slay them*" (Doctrine and Covenants 89:18–21; emphasis added).

The thirteenth article of faith, as written by Joseph Smith, also gives some instruction on how members of the Church should act: "We believe in being honest, true, chaste, benevolent, virtuous, and in doing good to all men; indeed, we may say that we follow the admonition of Paul—We believe all things, we hope all things, we have endured many things, and hope to be able to endure all things. If there is anything virtuous, lovely, or of good report or praiseworthy, we seek after these things."

One of the vital elements of the mission of The Church of Jesus Christ of Latter-day Saints is the care of the poor and needy. To help achieve this end, the Church Welfare Plan was established in 1936. Members of the Church are encouraged to abstain from food and drink for twenty-four hours on the first Sunday of the month (called fast Sunday). They are asked to contribute the equivalent of the cost of those meals (or much more, if they are in a position to do so) to what is called the Fast Offering fund. This money is used by the bishop (pastor) to help members of the local ward or branch (congregation or parish) who are unable to meet their own needs for food, rent or mortgage payments, and health challenges. If this money is not all used by the ward, the remainder is then passed along to the stake (diocese), where it may be used for needy people in other wards.

In 1842 Joseph Smith wrote that a member of the restored Church "is to feed the hungry, to clothe the naked, to provide for the widow, to dry up the tear of the orphan, to comfort the afflicted, *whether in this church, or in any other, or in no church at all*, wherever he finds them."[2] Members of the Church who are in a position to do so may contribute to the Church Humanitarian Fund, which is used to meet the needs of the suffering throughout the world of *those who are not Latter-day Saints*. One Church leader made this report to the members of the Church in a general conference: "I am reporting back to you about how The Church of Jesus Christ of Latter-day Saints is responding to hurricanes, earthquakes, refugee displacement—and even a pandemic—thanks to the kindness of the Latter-day Saints and many friends. While the more than 1,500 COVID-19 projects were certainly the largest focus of the Church's relief over the last 18 months, the Church also responded to 933 natural disasters and refugee crises in 108 countries."[3]

---

2. *Teachings of Presidents of the Church: Joseph Smith* (Salt Lake City: The Church of Jesus Christ of Latter-day Saints, 2007), 426.
3. Ronald A. Rasband, "To Heal the World," *Liahona*, May 2022, 91.

8

Areas Where Latter-day Saint Practices Differ

By Dr. Robert L. Millet

An Individual Faith

In chapter 6, Dr. Mouw told the story of a man in a hotel room who was troubled and burdened with serious sin. If I understand this correctly, Evangelicals would speak of this man as having been "saved" or "born again." At the April 1998 general conference, President Dallin H. Oaks spoke of six different meanings of the words "saved" or "salvation": (1) being saved from the permanence of physical death through the Resurrection; (2) being saved from sin conditionally through being born again; (3) being saved from the darkness of ignorance of God and Christ concerning the purpose of life and the destiny of men and women; (4) being saved from the second death, the final spiritual death; (5) being saved to inherit a kingdom of glory hereafter; (6) being saved in the sense of gaining eternal life and exaltation.

Most Latter-day Saints would speak of the man in the hotel room being saved in the sense that he recognized and acknowledged his sinfulness and turned to Jesus Christ for divine help. Regarding the matter of being born again, Joseph Smith referred to the conversation between Jesus and

Nicodemus. In John 3:3, the Savior explained that a person must first be born again to *see* the kingdom of God—they must have a change of heart and must have their spiritual eyes opened to receive the truth. In this case, they must understand that salvation can come only through the Person and atoning work of Jesus Christ.

Second, John 3:5 indicates that a person must be born of water and of the Spirit in order to *enter* the kingdom of God. That is, Latter-day Saints believe and teach that a person must be (1) baptized (immersed) in water; and (2) confirmed and receive the gift of the Holy Ghost by the laying on of hands. Both ordinances must be performed by those holding proper priesthood authority. Joseph Smith also taught that the baptism of water is but half a baptism; we might as well baptize a bag of sand if we baptize a person and do not bestow upon him or her the gift of the Holy Ghost. We would thus speak of the baptism of water, followed by the baptism of fire or the Holy Ghost. In light of the above, I would say that the man in the hotel was born again to *see* the kingdom of God. In order to *enter*, he would need to be baptized and confirmed.

Sacraments or Ordinances

From a Latter-day Saint perspective, a sacrament is any action or rite performed by individuals that would draw them closer to God. For us, *sacraments* would include prayer, scripture study, fasting, Christlike service, exercising faith, repenting, priesthood blessings, receiving a patriarchal blessing, the ordinances of the gospel, and many other spiritual exercises. *Ordinances* are rites or ceremonies performed by the authority of the priesthood. For Latter-day Saints, the ordinances required for salvation include baptism, confirmation for the reception of the Spirit, and ordination to the priesthood for males. The ordinances of exaltation (salvation or eternal life, including the eternal continuation of the family) include the ordinances performed in the temple for both the living and the dead—the temple endowment, eternal marriage, and sealings of parents and children. From our perspective, all ordinances are sacraments, but not all sacraments are ordinances.

Covenants and ordinances receive a great deal of attention within the restored Church. The Saints are repeatedly encouraged to keep their covenants and be true to their sacred promises. When it comes to ordinances, it is not just the ceremony, the performance of a ritual, that is important. The ordinances of the gospel become channels of divine grace, channels of spiritual power. In speaking of the higher or Melchizedek Priesthood, a modern revelation states: "And this greater priesthood administereth the gospel and holdeth the key of the mysteries of the kingdom, even the key of the knowledge of God. Therefore, *in the ordinances thereof, the power of godliness is manifest*" (Doctrine and Covenants 84:19-20; emphasis added).

A specific example of a difference with our Evangelical brothers and sisters is the ordinance of baptism. As Dr. Mouw mentioned, because Evangelicals do not believe that anything can be required for salvation above and beyond the atoning sacrifice of the Savior, baptism is not a required ordinance.

In August of 1997, I was serving as dean of Religious Education at BYU. My associate dean, Brent Top, and I traveled with two Evangelical pastors to California to meet a prominent preacher-teacher. In the Sunday morning church service, the minister greeted the people but then began to chasten those who had been attending church services there over an extended period of time but had not been baptized. He spoke of how very important it was to be baptized.

After the service, we were able to meet and converse with the pastor of the congregation for a few minutes. The four of us then made our way to the car and began our drive back to the motel where we were staying. I asked our two Evangelical friends, "Is baptism essential for salvation, or isn't it? The pastor certainly sounded like it was essential." There was a short pause and then one of them replied, "Well, baptism is necessary but not essential." My associate and I looked at each other quizzically, and I then responded: "Would you like to tease that out? I mean, what is the difference between *essential* and *necessary*?" The other Evangelical explained that while baptism cannot be essential, every good Christian would want to be baptized. It's what Christians do.

Our Evangelical friends' position on why an ordinance like baptism cannot be *essential* is as follows: The only thing that is truly essential for salvation, from their perspective, is the atoning work of Jesus Christ; anything else would be supplementing what Jesus did and thereby declaring that His atoning suffering was not sufficient to save people. To say that baptism is necessary, from their perspective, is to say that serious Christians really should follow the example of Jesus and be baptized. A phrase I have heard many times is "a Christ supplemented is a Christ supplanted."

Church Life

An Evangelical who visits a Latter-day Saint sacrament meeting (the main worship service on the Sabbath) would recognize many similarities to their own faith and church life.

The main purpose for the meeting is the partaking of the bread and water in remembrance of the broken body and spilt blood of the Lord Jesus Christ. One main difference in the worship service has to do with the sermons that are offered. The Church of Jesus Christ of Latter-day Saints contains a lay ministry, which means there are no paid officers or pastors, no persons who have received formal theological training in order to be involved in the ministry.

Those called to serve in positions of authority or to teach or lead are members of the ward or congregation. That means that the bishop of the ward might work for a living as a plumber, an electrician, a university professor, or a scientist. While the bishop or one of his two counselors may occasionally speak in sacrament meeting, the talks or sermons are typically delivered by the members who have been invited by the bishopric to speak.

The hymns and sacred anthems sung by Latter-day Saints are very traditional, much of the lyrics and music having been written by persons of other faiths. While many of the hymns are also written by members of the restored Church, it is not uncommon for the Saints to sing hymns written or music composed by Charles Wesley, Johannes Bach, Mary Baker Eddy, Katherine Lee Bates, Bernard of Clairvaux, Phillips Brooks, Fanny Crosby, Rudyard Kipling, Martin Luther, John Henry Newman, John Newton, St. Francis of Assisi, Isaac Watts, and Ralph Vaughn Williams.

Hymns of worship or praise that are sung regularly include "Abide with Me," "All Glory, Laud, and Honor," "Behold the Great Redeemer Die," "Come unto Jesus," "Glory to God on High," "God Loved Us, So He sent His Son," "How Firm a Foundation," "How Great Thou Art," "I Know that My Redeemer Lives," "I Stand All Amazed," "Jesus of Nazareth, Savior and King," "More Holiness Give Me," "O Savior, Thou Who Wearest a Crown," "Rock of Ages," "A Mighty Fortress," "Jesus, the Very Thought of Thee," and scores of others.

Twice a year, during the first weekend of April and October, The Church of Jesus Christ of Latter-day Saints convenes a two-day general conference for all members of the Church throughout the world. The President of the Church, sustained by the Saints as a prophet, seer, and revelator, presides at the conference and usually speaks at least three times during the two days. Members of the Quorum of the Twelve Apostles each deliver a message, as do selected members of the Seventy. General leaders of the Church's organizations (Sunday School, Young Women, Primary, and Young Men) are also called upon to speak. Millions participate in general conference by being present in the 21,000-seat conference center in Salt Lake City or by television, radio, or online broadcasts. Sermons are delivered, principles and doctrine are discussed, policies or procedures are announced, and the members of the Church receive comfort and encouragement to be valiant in the testimony of Jesus. One former President of the Church, Harold B. Lee, counseled the Latter-day Saints to make the teachings of that particular conference their "walk and talk" for the next six months.

In teaching the Nephites in ancient America, the Risen Lord declared: "Behold I have given unto you my gospel, and this is the gospel which I have given unto you—that I came into the world to do the will of my Father, because my Father sent me. And my Father sent me that I might be lifted up upon the cross; and after that I had been lifted up upon the cross, that I might draw all men unto me." He then explained how an individual can draw upon His Infinite Atonement by repenting, being baptized by water, and then being baptized by the Spirit, that is, sanctified by the reception of the Holy Ghost. The Lord then stated: "Verily, verily, I say unto you, *this is my gospel*; and *ye know the things that ye must do in my church; for the works which ye have seen me do that shall ye also do*" (3 Nephi 27:13-14, 19-21; emphasis added). In short, the Church of Jesus Christ provides the means by which we as the Christian community can carry on the work of redemption that our Lord and Savior initiated through His sufferings and death. The Church represents the outworking, the means by which the teachings, service to others, and organized sacrifice are accomplished.

9

Appreciation for Evangelical Practices

By Dr. Robert L. Millet

Perhaps more than anything else, I have been deeply moved—in my decades-long engagement with Evangelicals—with just how Christ-centered Evangelical Christians tend to be. They love and adore Him, rejoice in Him, speak of Him often, and refer to Him as their Friend. They remark frequently of their "personal relationship with Jesus Christ," a reverential closeness that really ought to exist between the Savior of humankind and those who accept and confess Him, not only as their Savior and God but also as their Lord, the Master of their individual universe.

Linked with their adoration and devotion toward Christ is their undying trust in His merits, mercy, and grace. They have learned not to trust in their own good works for salvation but instead to rely on the saving and redemptive work of the Son of God. Those Evangelicals who understand their own doctrine know of the important place of the works of righteousness—not in any way as a means of salvation, but instead as a way of expressing eternal gratitude and love to Him who bought us with His blood.

I have been moved to the core with how my Evangelical brothers and sisters love the Holy Bible—how they quote from it, teach from it, and find ancient answers to current questions in it. I wish that my own people were more serious students of the Bible. More specifically, I wish more Latter-day Saints spent the time and put in the effort to understand and teach from the writings of the Apostle Paul as my Evangelical friends do. For too many Latter-day Saints, Paul remains a stranger, an enigma, and his epistles are too often viewed with confusion, reticence, even suspicion. In my many years of teaching Paul, I have witnessed how a surprising number of Latter-day Saints perceive him to be a kind of ancient Protestant. But the resurrected Savior said of the recently converted Saul of Tarsus that "he is a chosen vessel unto me" (Acts 9:15).

I have been deeply impressed with how my Evangelical associates look upon God and Christ with a profound sense of awe. Too often, that kind of devotion, that kind of reverence, is lacking among some of my own faith. I suppose because Latter-day Saints believe and teach that God is an exalted Man of Holiness and that he has a body of flesh and bones, there may not be that sacred inclination to think upon Him and approach Him with wonder and awe. I am particularly grateful, therefore, that the 1985 edition of the Latter-day Saint hymnal included the beloved Christian hymn "How Great Thou Art." I sense that it has helped many of us in the restored Church to acknowledge our absolute nothingness without the Almighty's tender mercy and amazing grace.

Surely part of coming to know our Lord and Savior is coming to know who He is and what He has done. The more we learn of Him, the more we search the prophets and pore over the revelations, the more I am persuaded that a major indicator of our spiritual development is the growing realization that Jesus Christ is God; that, under the direction of the Father, He is the Creator and Governor of all things; that His redemptive labors were infinite and eternal in scope; that He has power over life and death, power over the very elements that make up our world; that in a future day He will return to earth, this time in power and glory, and reign as King of kings and Lord of lords; and that in order to come unto Him and to *stand* before Him, we must first *fall to our knees* in an attitude of adoration, praise, awe, and worship. I admire and have a sense of "holy envy" toward my Evangelical friends who "do awe" toward our Heavenly Father and his Son, Jesus Christ, so naturally, so appropriately, so regularly.

Finally, I have learned much from my interfaith engagement with Evangelicals about the importance of having what they call eternal security—the assurance that because of their acceptance of and faith in the sufferings and death of Jesus Christ, they are saved. To be sure, as a Latter-day Saint, I believe that we may, as the Lord said in an early revelation, "fall from grace and depart from the living God," and that the Lord expects us to endure faithfully and keep our covenants to the end of our mortal lives. It is, however, as a result of my close encounter with dedicated and committed Evangelicals who feel a peaceful assurance concerning their salvation, that I have been highly motivated to search the scriptures and study the teachings of latter-day apostles and prophets to see if there is not a comparable sense of "eternal security" within our own doctrine.

As a result of my search, I first encountered Paul's insights into how we may receive the "earnest of our inheritance" (Ephesians 1:14) or the "earnest of the Spirit" (2 Corinthians 1:21–22). I came to understand more clearly that when we feel the Holy Ghost working within us, it is our Father in Heaven's way of letting us know that He is pleased with us, that we are spiritually on course, that we are in line to receive salvation or eternal life, the greatest of all the gifts of God. It is as if the presence of the Spirit is God's "earnest money" on us, a divine declaration that He seriously intends to "purchase" us, to save us. I also began to notice that some of our Church leaders have addressed this matter. Brigham Young, the second President of the restored Church, stated, "It is present salvation and the present influence of the Holy Ghost that we need every day to keep us on saving ground."[1] Similarly, David O. McKay, the Prophet of my boyhood, explained that the gospel of Jesus Christ makes available to every person "salvation *here*— here and now . . . as well as hereafter."[2] I suppose I might have stumbled upon such teachings if I had not been acquainted with the beliefs of my Evangelical friends, but maybe not. My effort to better understand the peaceful confidence they felt, and about which they spoke, motivated me to search for like teachings within the restored gospel. I found them, and they have been of inestimable worth to me and those I teach.

Finally, I want to express my "holy gratitude" for the privilege—and I count it as such—of meeting and coming to know and love my dear colleague and co-author, Richard J. Mouw. To me, he is the consummate Christian, a man possessed of a depth of commitment to his own faith and way of life, but also a rare person whose breadth and wideness of mercy I have not encountered very often in my life. In spite of his remarkably deep understanding and grasp of the history and theology of Christianity, he is of that rare breed of human being whose brilliance is only surpassed by

---

1. *Journal of Discourses,* 26 vols. (Liverpool: F. D. Richards & Sons, 1851-86), 8:124-25.
2. David O. McKay, *Gospel Ideals* (Salt Lake City: The Improvement Era, 1953), 6.

his humility—his willingness to consider carefully other points of view, to acknowledge goodness and truth when he sees it, to admit that he doesn't have all the answers but is eager to learn more.

I can still recall vividly a poignant moment in the midst of our Latter-day Saint–Evangelical dialogue when we were engaged in an intense discussion of the doctrine of the Trinity/Godhead. It was, in fact, the second two-day session where this most difficult and complex matter was considered. The intensity was not a product of argument or debate but rather a serious engagement with a heavy and crucial doctrinal matter. There was a pause in the dialogue that lasted for about one minute. Dr. Mouw then spoke up and asked a question of his Evangelical colleagues, something like the following: "Are we Evangelicals so sure, so confident, so knowledgeable of the nature of Almighty God that we can declare that our Latter-day Saint colleagues are wrong?" It was a moment of sweet humility, tender earnestness on the part of my dear friend that speaks volumes about his goodness and his Christian character. My decades-long association with him has been one of the rich blessings of my life, one for which I will be forever grateful.

SECTION 3
Interfaith Dialogue

10

Latter-day Saint Engagement with Evangelicalism

By Dr. Richard J. Mouw and Dr. Robert L. Millet

It is tragic that religious discussions with those of other faiths too often devolve into debates or arguments over who is right and who is wrong. This need not happen when men and women of good will come together in an attitude of openness and in a sincere effort to better understand and be understood. Winning a friend is so much more enjoyable and soul-satisfying than winning an argument.

Currently we face tremendous challenges in our world—divorce, fatherless homes, poverty, child and spouse abuse, pornography, spreading crime and delinquency, racial unrest, and wars. It seems foolish for men and women who believe in God and profess a belief in Jesus Christ as Savior and Redeemer to allow doctrinal differences to prevent them from becoming better acquainted and eventually working together to perpetuate those time-honored values that are the foundation of a great society.

In addressing the Board of the National Association of Evangelicals in March of 2011, Elder Jeffrey R. Holland stated: "Friends, you know what I know—that there is in the modern world so much sin and moral decay affecting everyone, especially the young, and it seems to be getting worse by the day. . . . Surely there is a way for people of good will who love God and have taken upon themselves the name of Christ to stand together . . . for the cause of Christ and against the forces of sin. In this we have every right to be bold and believing, for 'if God be for us, who can be against us?'"[1]

We have learned by many years of experience that people can be committed to the beliefs and practices of their particular church, synagogue, mosque, or temple and, at the same time, reach out to people who believe differently than they do, without compromising one whit of their beliefs or way of life. We are who we are, and we believe what we believe. There is, however, something much deeper within us than our religious beliefs—namely, our *shared humanity*. We are all children of the same God, and, in that sense, members of the same family. Sibling rivalry of this sort must pain our Lord and Savior, for it was at the close of His ministry that He charged His disciples to strive to be one, even as He and His Father are one (John 17:20–23).

In this spirit a group of six Evangelical Christian professors and six Latter-day Saint professors met in Provo, Utah, for the first time in May of 2000 for what came to be known as the Mormon–Evangelical Dialogue. In that first meeting, there was a bit of tension in the air, not negative feelings since everyone was very friendly, but a bit of uneasiness as to where this meeting would go. What would be the objective? Was it about conversion? We conversed for two days on many topics, and the purposes of the dialogue gradually began to take shape. Over the years we have discussed such matters as the earliest Christian teachings about Jesus, Atonement of and salvation in Christ, grace and works, the Fall, Joseph Smith, Joseph's First Vision, scripture, revelation, spiritual gifts, authority, God, Godhead/Trinity, and *theosis*/deification. What a journey!

Richard J. Mouw, at the time President of Fuller Theological Seminary in Pasadena, California, was their group's leader, and Robert L. Millet took responsibility for gathering the Latter-day Saint contingent. We decided that we would meet twice each year and alternate venues between Pasadena and Provo. Each time we met we would discuss a doctrinal topic. In preparation for such a dialogue, we would read Latter-day Saint writings on the subject and Evangelical or traditional Christian materials. One of the things that

---

1. Jeffrey R. Holland, "Standing Together for the Cause of Christ," in *To My Friends: Messages of Counsel and Comfort* (Salt Lake City: Deseret Book, 2014), 121–22.

made this dialogue particularly interesting is that Evangelical Christians and Latter-day Saints have not exactly been close friends through the years! Rather, we have too often been one another's bitterest enemies.

We were only into this endeavor a year or two before it was obvious that something curious and rather touching was taking place: deep friendships were being formed; respect and love were developing among the members of the group.

About five or six years into the dialogue, and just as we were preparing to leave for home on the third day of our meetings, I (Robert) said: "Okay everyone, before we split up, let's remember that our topic for next time is _____ and that we'll be meeting in Provo." At that point, Richard Mouw said, "Bob, about that—we don't want to meet in Provo. We love Provo, but we want to meet in Nauvoo, Illinois." And so we did. Two or three years later Richard said, "We want to meet in Palmyra, New York." So, we met in Palmyra and spent several days discussing the beginnings of The Church of Jesus Christ of Latter-day Saints.

We eventually met in Kirtland, Ohio. Our reading in preparation for our Kirtland dialogue was spiritual gifts. The Latter-day Saints spoke at some length about the Pentecostal outpouring of the Spirit that took place in and around the dedication of the Kirtland Temple in 1836. In American Christianity, in the first decade of the twentieth century, a group of Christian seekers began to speak in tongues in a home on Azusa Street in Los Angeles. That's the beginning of what is now called the Pentecostal movement, tongues being one of their most prominent spiritual gifts. It was surprising for our Evangelical colleagues to learn that Latter-day Saints were speaking in tongues some seventy years before the Azusa Street Revival.

From the beginning of the dialogue, we agreed that this was not to be a debate or an argument. We were not doing apologetics—defending our faith through proving the other guy wrong. It was not necessary for us to agree on all matters of doctrine. We are who we are, and we believe what we believe. This was to be a dialogue, a conversation intended to build understanding and foster friendships between our two faiths. It was also intended to alleviate misunderstanding and avoid misrepresentation in the future. Early on in our conversations, Richard made the comment, "We're not going to ask the Latter-day Saints to prove to us that Moroni brought golden plates to Joseph Smith any more than if I were in dialogue with Muslims, I would demand that they prove to me that the angel Gabriel came down and dictated the

Quran to Mohammad. Those are their holy books, and that's just a given. Let's move on."

We live in a world today where moral and family values are being challenged, threatened, and in some ways discarded. We need to develop the kind of relationships with other faiths that would enable us to cooperate with those whose values are like our own, to work harmoniously in upholding time-honored values and absolute truths, as well as defending the religious liberties that have helped to make this nation great.

As the years passed and as our love and admiration for one another grew, many of us came to appreciate a scriptural passage from the New Testament more and more. Jesus taught: "Where two or three are gathered together in my name, there am I in the midst of them" (Matthew 18:20). It felt like every time we met we could feel a divine, superintending Presence through these lengthy conversations. Our hearts were inspired, our souls comforted, and our understanding expanded. This wasn't just an intellectual exercise; we were growing in ways that are spiritually healthy. As much as the two of us have enjoyed teaching, research, and writing in our academic pursuits, in many ways the most rewarding work with which we have been involved has been interfaith engagement.

One of the things that made this dialogue so fascinating is that Evangelical Christians and Latter-day Saints have in the past acted as though we were one another's bitterest enemy. And this is what has made the formation of valued associations so interesting: unity and friendship developed, in spite of what has gone on between us in the past. It is extremely hard to name-call, pigeon-hole, categorize, or even demonize someone who has become a valued friend or trusted colleague.

In so many ways, we agree on matters of great importance:

- We believe in God, our Father in Heaven, and that He has a plan for the happiness and salvation of all His children.
- We believe that Jesus Christ is the Son of God and the Savior of all humanity, and that salvation comes only through believing in Him and accepting His gospel.
- We want the best possible world to pass on to our children and grandchildren. If we allow our theological differences or suspicions to prevent us from working together to improve society, everyone loses, which means that Satan wins.
- We are concerned about the gradual erosion of our religious liberties.

Religion and religious discourse have been pushed to the margins of our society. Many have taken the position that if people are especially devout in their faith that such persons are at best irrational and at worst dangerous.

- As religion, religious values, and religious discourse are excluded from the public square, the success of families declines. At the same time, as families and family life are disrupted or undermined, religion and religious values begin to be discarded or ignored.

- Persons in our society who now identify themselves as "nones" or "dones"—those who have no religious affiliation, who have cut all ties with the institutional church, who speak of themselves as "spiritual but not religious"—constitute almost 30 percent of the American population. In other words, our nation is in the midst of a massive and ever-spreading crisis of faith. Members of all religious denominations must work together to find solutions to stem the tide of this spiritual pandemic.

The God we worship is the God of all creation, an infinite, eternal, and omni-loving Being who will do all that He can to inspire, lift, and bring greater light into the lives of His children. He is the only true God and thus the only living Deity who can hear and respond to the earnest petitions of His children. He loves us all and is pleased with any and every halting effort on our part to learn of Him, serve Him, and be true to His light within us. In a significant address given at the University of Southern California, Elder Dieter F. Uchtdorf, one of the apostles of The Church of Jesus Christ of Latter-day Saints, stated: "The effort to throw off traditions of distrust and pettiness and truly see one another with new eyes—to see each other not as aliens or adversaries but as fellow travelers, brothers and sisters, and children of God—is one of the most challenging while at the same time most rewarding and ennobling experiences of our human existence."[2]

---

2. Dieter F. Uchtdorf, "Fellow Travelers, Brothers and Sisters, Children of God," address delivered at the inaugural symposium of the John A. Widtsoe Foundation, University of Southern California, April 24, 2015.

11

Appreciation for Latter-day Saint Beliefs and Practices

By Dr. Richard J. Mouw

"Holy envy" toward Latter-day Saints has been a rare thing in the history of encounters between Evangelicals and Latter-day Saints. There has been, however, considerable envy of the not-so-holy variety. It is the kind of competitive spirit that characterizes relations between, say, the Boston Red Sox and the New York Yankees. They grudgingly respect each other's prowess and work hard to match each other's skills—but all for the purpose of outdoing the other.

The unfriendly relations between Evangelicals and Latter-day Saints go back to the beginnings of our shared history. While Catholics and the more liberal Protestant (mainline) denominations have, for the most part, not paid much attention to the teachings of The Church of Jesus Christ of Latter-day Saints, evangelicals nurtured a strong hostility toward Joseph Smith and his followers, typically treating it as one of the more dangerous of the American cults. Evangelicals have grown in their worries as the Latter-day Saints have transitioned from being a home-grown movement to an international religion. Like the Latter-day Saints, Evangelicalism has also experienced major growth in the southern hemisphere in recent decades, and in each case the growth has been due to a passionate commitment to

Evangelism or missionary activity. The relationship has been complicated by the fact that often missionaries from the two movements show up in the same region.

The fact that Evangelicals have seen the Latter-day Saint movement as a threat has resulted in sustained attacks against them by Evangelicals—often taking the form of "exposes" regarding events and practices in Latter-day Saint history. An influential twentieth-century Evangelical leader in these attacks was Walter Martin, who wrote some best-selling books, *The Rise of the Cults* (1957) and *The Kingdom of the Cults* (1966), where he depicted The Church of Jesus Christ of Latter-day Saints as an especially dangerous religious movement. Martin's efforts—he was also a popular speaker in local congregations—spawned an active "counter-cult" movement. That movement gained further strength from the 1982 film, *The God Makers*, produced by Dave Hunt and Ed Decker, who followed up with a widely read book by the same title.

These Evangelical critics have often treated accounts of the origins of The Church of Jesus Christ of Latter-day Saints in terms of deception, even Satanic influence. Others have focused on demonstrating how Latter-day Saint teaching constitutes a grand scale departure from historic Christian doctrines. This is exemplified in an observation I read recently by an Evangelical theologian who said that "Mormonism differs profoundly from orthodox Christianity on almost every point—its understanding of God, mankind, Jesus, the Bible, sin, salvation, and hell."

It should be clear from what I have written in previous sections of this book that I regret the Evangelical attack mode. My own understanding of Latter-day Saint life and thought, based on much study and dialogue over the past two decades, does not leave me with the notion of an unbridgeable gap between us. Indeed, to put it in personal terms, while Robert Millet and I have serious disagreements about key theological teachings, I consider him to be a dear brother in Christ.

So here are some of the "holy envy" elements in my experiences with Latter-day Saints. I'll start with two items where many Evangelicals, who otherwise might manifest hostility toward Latter-day Saints, will be inclined to express genuine appreciation—even though the commendations may fall short of being of a "holy" status. One is music. Evangelicals love hymns of praise, and we buy many recordings of the Tabernacle Choir at Temple Square. A second area has to do with family values. On this topic we have come a long way: having once strongly condemned Latter-day Saint plural marriage as a willful attempt to undercut divinely revealed norms for marriage and parenting, these days many Evangelicals see the Latter-day Saints as allies in "culture war" struggles with secularist departures from traditional patterns of family life.

My own personal words of praise—shared by my Evangelical co-participants in our decades of formal dialogue—go much further into the realm of the holy. One significant element in my appreciation for the Latter-day Saints is the very thing I mentioned as a key source of tension between our communities—the Latter-day Saints' missionary passion. To be sure, it is painful for both sides when we find ourselves in situations where we are competing for the same souls. But we also bring our message to different populations, and I have read enough testimonies from Latter-day Saint converts around the world to be assured that there are people who come to a genuine faith in Jesus Christ through the efforts of Latter-day Saint missionaries. For this I am deeply grateful.

Another matter of holy envy for me is the strong Latter-day Saint sense of sacred places. Most of our dialogue events have been held at either the campus of Fuller Theological Seminary in Pasadena, California, or at Brigham Young University in Provo, Utah. In addition, as Robert noted above, we have held meetings, in Palmyra, Kirtland, and Nauvoo. In one of our planning sessions Robert Millet wondered whether we should schedule a time at an Evangelical sacred site. My response was that we don't have any sacred sites. We then decided, at Robert's suggestion, to meet at Wheaton College in Illinois, with side trips to the Moody Bible Institute and the Pacific Garden Mission in the Chicago area. Those places have historic significance for the Evangelical movement, but they lack the sacred aura of Latter-day Saint places like the grove in Palmyra, the temple in Kirtland, and the banks of the Mississippi River in Nauvoo. For me, though, one of the most moving experiences was sitting in the cell of the Carthage, Illinois, jail, having a tearful time of prayer where Joseph Smith and his brother Hyrum were murdered in June of 1844.

Once I was traveling across New York State and decided to take a break by stopping off at Palmyra. As I sat on a bench in the Sacred Grove, a father and a young son walked by. I heard the boy ask in a hushed voice, "Is this where it happened, Daddy?" His father responded in an equally quiet tone, "We don't know the exact spot, but we are near. We'll walk a little further and then we'll stop to pray." It struck me that I knew of no place in America where an Evangelical father and son could have had that reverent exchange. I envied them.

As an academic, I also have great respect and appreciation for Latter-day Saint scholarship. Our dialogues have motivated me to read widely in Latter-day Saint history, and I am deeply impressed by the honesty of Latter-day Saint scholars in the detailed manner in which they explore their church's history. I have also been inspired by Latter-day Saint devotional writing. I have not only benefited from the printed page, but I have also been greatly enriched by attending conferences organized by my Latter-day Saint friends. These experiences have been enhanced by opportunities to spend time—often as a guest speaker—at Latter-day Saint Institutes of Religion and in extensive conversations with faculty and students at Brigham Young University.

A final matter that I must mention may seem a bit odd coming from an Evangelical: I have experienced holy envy when watching recordings of the Church's general conferences. I am impressed with the General Authorities' presentations. I love Elder Jeffrey Holland's inspiring April 2009 address, "None Were with Him," which reverently addressed the Savior's excruciatingly painful hours on the cross of Calvary. I have returned to that message, as well as others, several times. The Latter-day Saint leadership uses general conference for timely, thoughtful, and inspirational teaching that doesn't just apply to members of the Church.

Earlier in this book I mentioned the significance of the parachurch phenomenon in Evangelicalism. Obviously, I approve of that way of relating to each other in our Evangelical movement. There is, however, something marvelous about the Saints' general conference, a gathering of a global church, a virtual assembly called together to affirm shared beliefs and commitments. I know that I too have been taught on these occasions, and am blessed to bear witness with my brother Robert Millet that our two communities have much to learn from each other. May that continue to happen, by God's grace!

APPENDICES

Glossary of Evangelical Terms

apologists: those involved in the defense of the Christian faith.

arianism: the belief that Jesus Christ is subordinate to the Father, the highest created being of God.

Arminianism: the teachings of Jacob Arminius (ca. 335–336) that opposed the Calvinist doctrine of predestination. Arminius taught that salvation is freely chosen and can be freely lost; a person can "fall from grace."

Bible Institute: typically a three to four year college-level institution, emphasizing "practical training" in Christianity. The Moody Bible Institute in Chicago is perhaps the best known.

born again: a common Evangelical term taken from John 3:3: "Ye must be born again," denoting a person coming to have a personal relationship with Jesus Christ.

Calvinism: the doctrine set forth by John Calvin (1509–1564) concerning the complete sovereignty of God. Over the years, Calvinism has been characterized as consisting of five beliefs, best explained through the acronym TULIP—Total depravity; Unconditional election to eternal life (predestination); Limited Atonement (only efficacious for those who are elect); Irresistible grace (that the Holy Spirit will work upon the hearts of the elect, such that they cannot resist God's saving grace); Perseverance of the Saints (one cannot fall from grace).

Charismatic Christians: those who believe in and enjoy the gifts of the Spirit (particularly tongues, healing, miracles).

Charismatic Renewal: a movement, begun in the 1950s, of Pentecostal-type emphases among mainline Protestants and Catholics, featuring "tongue-speaking" and being "filled with the Holy Spirit."

conditional immortality: the belief that those who do not accept Jesus Christ and the salvation He offers will, after death, cease to exist; sometimes referred to as annihilationism.

consubstantiation: a belief of Martin Luther and his followers that Jesus Christ is "present in" the emblems of the sacrament.

creatio ex nihilo: the belief that all things were created "out of nothing."

ecclesiology: the study of matters pertaining to the church.

eschatology: the theological study of "last things" or "end times," focusing on the nature of the afterlife and the biblical portrayals of how human history as we know it will come to an end.

Eucharist: the sacrament of the Lord's Supper, also known as Communion.

general revelation: the manner in which God conveys or reveals to all men and women the power to reason and a conscience to distinguish good from evil. This may be what Latter-day Saints call the Light of Christ or Spirit of Jesus Christ; to be distinguished from special revelation.

glossolalia: speaking in tongues.

grace: unearned divine assistance, unmerited divine favor, heavenly help.

Holiness Movement: a movement during the nineteenth century by those who were followers of John Wesley to strive for "entire sanctification"—to become pure and sin-resistant.

homoousious: a Greek term used in the Nicene Council (AD 325) to express that the Father, the Son, and the Holy Spirit are of the "same substance" or "same essence." They are one being, one God.

homoiousios: a Greek term used by some early Christians that means "of similar substance."

impassibility: a belief that God is unaffected by earthly circumstances, including human suffering; He cannot change in any way.

imputation: the notion that when one comes unto Christ by faith he or she is justified by God and that the righteousness of Christ is imputed or put on his or her spiritual account. It is not the individual's righteousness, but the righteousness of the Savior.

incarnation: the coming of God to earth to take a physical body; what Latter-day Saints would call the condescension of God.

inerrancy: the view that the Bible is "without error," allowing for copying mistakes made since the time of the "original manuscripts." Controversies about this teaching among Evangelicals have focused on whether inerrancy applies to divine revelation about "faith and life," or whether it applies also to historical and scientific details.

justification: the means by which a person is forgiven, pardoned, exonerated, and placed in proper relationship with God.

Limited Atonement: the belief that the blessings of the Atonement of Jesus Christ are only extended to the elect, those chosen for eternal life before they were born; also called "particular redemption."

modalism: a heresy on the part of those who conceive of the Trinity or Godhead as consisting of three different modes or representations of God, three faces of the same Being.

monotheism: the belief in one God, not three or many. The Father, Son, and Holy Spirit are believed to be different persons but the same Being, the same God.

Nicene Creed: the document produced in AD 325 by a gathering of more than three hundred bishops of the church in their effort to better understand and explain the nature of God and the proper relationship of all three members of the Godhead or Trinity.

original sin: the taint of sin answered upon all of the descendants of Adam and Eve because of the rebellion of our first parents and their partaking of the forbidden fruit in the Garden of Eden.

Parousia: the Second Coming of Jesus Christ, when He will be present with earth's inhabitants once more.

penal substitution: the idea that Jesus Christ took upon Him the weight and burden of our sins and became "sin for us" (2 Corinthians 5:21); He was exposed to the wrath of God that would otherwise be answered upon all the descendants of Adam and Eve; He stood in our place.

Orthodox: a word that literally means "right walk"; it refers to accurate or correct teaching of doctrine, as opposed to the unorthodox or heretical.

pneumatology: the study of the Holy Spirit.

prevenient grace: a "coming before" grace; God's work upon His children through the Holy Spirit to prepare them for the receipt of the gospel of Jesus Christ.

priesthood of believers: the belief, put forward by leaders of the Protestant Reformation, that anyone who comes unto Christ and enjoys His redeeming power in his or her life becomes a priest; thus no one stands between them and Deity. This was a reaction to what the Reformers felt to be the abuses of the Roman Catholic priesthood.

rapture: a belief that faithful Christians will be lifted up or "caught up" to meet Jesus when he returns in glory.

regeneration: what happens in the internal life of a person who becomes a Christian. This is a technical term for being "born again."

sanctification: the gradual process in the Christian life of an individual growing into holiness.

seminary: a graduate school for the study of theological subjects, typically centered on preparation for leadership in church ministry.

soteriology: the subdivision of theology that focuses on the nature of salvation.

special revelation: divine inspiration that pertains to being saved through Jesus Christ, above and beyond general revelation.

theodicy: an effort to address the problem of reconciling the omnipotence and omni-loving nature of Deity with the evil and human suffering that prevail in the world.

transubstantiation: a Roman Catholic belief that the emblems of the sacrament are transformed into the actual body and blood of Christ.

Trinity: the members of the Godhead. The doctrine of the Trinity is the teaching that the Father, Son, and Holy Ghost are one is substance, one in essence, three divine Persons but one Being, one God.

unconditional election: the notion that people are predestined to salvation from the foundation of the world; these are the elect, while all others are the reprobate.

universalism: the belief that because God possesses all of the divine attributes in perfection, including patience, he will eventually save all of His children.

Prominent Evangelical Figures

Craig L. Blomberg (1955–): distinguished professor emeritus of New Testament at Denver Seminary, Blomberg was the co-author with Stephen Robinson of *How Wide the Divide? A Mormon and an Evangelical in Dialogue*. He has lectured widely on six continents.

Francis Collins (1950–): Evangelical scientist who headed up the Human Genome Project and served within the National Institute of Health in three presidential administrations. Highly regarded speaker and writer on topics dealing with faith and science.

Rachel den Hollander (1984–): Evangelical attorney and outspoken advocate for women who have been abused in athletic and church/religious contexts. She herself was abused by a coach during her time as a gymnast.

Jerry Falwell Sr. (1933–2007): the late Evangelical founder of the Moral Majority and chancellor at Liberty University.

Billy Graham (1918–2018): the most influential and successful evangelist of the twentieth century. While ordained as a Southern Baptist, William Franklin Graham—always known as Billy—was widely respected across denominational and international and interfaith lines. He was also an unofficial spiritual adviser to several presidents of the United States.

Nathan Hatch (1946–): Evangelical historian who served as Provost at the University of Notre Dame before becoming President of Wake Forest

University. He is recognized as one of the most prominent American religious historians.

Carl F. H. Henry (1913–2003): the most prominent Evangelical theologian of the post-World War II era. Founding editor of the magazine *Christianity Today*.

Bob Jones (1883–1968): the founder and president of Bob Jones University. He was an outspoken Fundamentalist leader, known for his segregationist views and his criticisms of Billy Graham for cooperating with liberals and Catholics.

J. Gresham Machen (1881–1937): a professor at Princeton Theological Seminary who established the theologically conservative Westminster Theological Seminary in Philadelphia.

George Marsden (1939–): Evangelical historian who taught and researched at Calvin College and later at the University of Notre Dame. He is the author of a ground-breaking history of Fundamentalism, as well as of an award-winning biography of the Puritan theologian Jonathan Edwards.

Walter Martin (1928–1989): a leading voice in the "counter-cult" movement, known for his strident opposition to The Church of Jesus Christ of Latter-day Saints, which he viewed as Satan-inspired. His most famous publication is *Kingdom of the Cults*.

Dwight L. Moody (1837–1899): a beloved and revered American evangelist whose teachings and writings are still relied upon heavily. He was responsible for the establishment of Moody Church, Moody Bible Institute, Moody Publishers, and Mount Hermon School in Massachusetts.

Beth Moore (1957–): Wanda Elizabeth Moore, an American evangelist, author, and Bible teacher. She is the president of Living Proof Ministries, a Christian organization which she founded in 1994 with the purpose of teaching women to know and love Jesus through the study of scripture.

Russell Moore (1971–): Evangelical theologian and political commentator who led the Southern Baptist Convention's Ethics and Religious Liberty Commission in Washington, D.C., from 2013 to 2021. He resigned in opposition to "extremist" social political views in the denomination. He was appointed as director of the Public Theology Project at *Christianity Today* and later became the editor-in-chief of *Christianity Today*.

Mark Noll (1946–): historian of American religion who taught at Wheaton College, where he co-founded the Institute for the Study of Evangelicalism. He later joined the history faculty at the University of Notre Dame. He was included in *Time* magazine's 2005 list of most influential Evangelicals.

Harold John Ockenga (1905–1985): longtime pastor at Boston's Park Street Church, he also served twice as President of Fuller Theological Seminary and Gordon-Conwell Theological Seminary. Ockenga was also the founder in the post-World War II era of the National Association of Evangelicals.

J. I. Packer (1926–2020): a prominent and beloved English-born and Canadian academic and churchman. He was one of the most influential Evangelicals in North America, known especially for his best-selling book, *Knowing God*, as well as his work as editor of the English Standard Version of the Bible.

Pat Robertson (1930–): one of the most famous entrepreneurial televangelists who founded The Christian Broadcasting Network and Regent University. He also hosted *The 700 Club*, where he often offered controversial political commentary. In 1988 he ran in the Republican primaries as a presidential candidate.

John Stott (1921–2011): one of the most beloved and respected Evangelical theologians of the twentieth century. He was an English Anglican pastor as well as an academic who authored more than fifty books, many of which have been translated into Chinese, Korean, and Spanish.

Philip Yancey (1949–): an American journalist who later chose to direct his writings to Christian audiences. His books have sold more than 15 million copies and have been translated into forty languages. A theme common to many of his works is the problem of evil and suffering in the world.

Suggested Readings

Balmer, Randall. *Blessed Assurance: A History of Evangelicalism in America.* Boston, MA: Beacon Press, 1999.

_____. *Mine Eyes Have Seen the Glory: A Journey into the Evangelical Subculture in America.* 3rd ed. New York: Oxford University Press, 2000.

Blomberg, Craig L and Stephen E. Robinson. *How Wide the Divide? A Mormon and an Evangelical in Conversation.* Downers Grove, IL: InterVarsity Press, 1997.

Graham, Billy. *Just as I Am: The Autobiography of Billy Graham.* Grand Rapids, MI: Zondervan, 1997.

Grenz, Stanley J., David Guretzki, and Cherith Fee Nordling, *Pocket Dictionary of Theological Terms.* Downers Grove, IL: InterVarsity Press, 1999.

Larsen, Timothy, David Bebbington, and Mark A. Noll, eds. *Biographical Dictionary of Evangelicals.* Downers Grove, IL: InterVarsity Press, 2003.

Marsden, George M. *Understanding Fundamentalism and Evangelicalism.* Grand Rapids, MI: Eerdmans, 1991.

McDermott, Gerald R., ed. *The Oxford Handbook of Evangelical Theology.* New York: Oxford University Press, 2010.

Millet, Robert L. and Gerald R. McDermott. *Claiming Christ: A Mormon-Evangelical Debate*. Grand Rapids, MI: Brazos Press, 2007.

Millet, Robert L. and Gregory C. V. Johnson. *Bridging the Divide: The Continuing Conversation between a Mormon and an Evangelical*. Rhinebeck, NY: Monkfish Book Publishing Company, 2007.

Mouw, Richard J. *Adventures in Evangelical Civility: A Lifelong Quest for Common Ground*. Grand Rapids, MI: Brazos Press, 2016.

_____. *Talking with Mormons: An Invitation to Evangelicals*. Grand Rapids, MI: Eerdmans, 2012.

_____. *Uncommon Decency: Christian Civility in an Uncivil World*, rev. ed. Downers Grove, IL: InterVarsity Press, 2010.

Mouw, Richard J. and Robert L. Millet, eds. *Talking Doctrine: Mormons and Evangelicals in Conversation*. Downers Grove, IL: InterVarsity Press, 2015.

About the Authors

Richard J. Mouw

Richard J. Mouw was raised by an Evangelical pastor, and both he and his parents fully expected that he would follow his father's career path. During his undergraduate studies, Richard discovered that he loved the world of ideas and decided—much to the consternation of his parents—to aim at an academic vocation.

Richard earned a master's degree in philosophy from the University of Alberta in western Canada and a PhD from the University of Chicago. His first full-time teaching position was in the philosophy department at Calvin College (now Calvin University) in Grand Rapids, Michigan, and after seventeen years he joined the faculty at Fuller Theological Seminary in Southern California. He was later appointed provost and then president, and served in the latter capacity for twenty years. He is now fully retired from Fuller and is presently Senior Research Fellow in Faith and Politics at Calvin University.

His intellectual and spiritual journey has been greatly enhanced by dialogue with persons from other faith traditions. He has been especially blessed by the opportunities to be in sustained dialogue with Latter-day Saints, particularly with his dear friend, Robert Millet. He is deeply grateful for the opportunity to continue the conversation with him in this book.

Robert L. Millet

Robert Millet was born and raised in Baton Rouge, Louisiana. Following a full-time mission in the Eastern States Mission, he attended Brigham Young University, where he completed both bachelors and masters degrees in psychology.

Robert worked for LDS Social Services (now Family Services) as a marriage and family counselor before becoming a full-time seminary teacher. He later served as director of the Institute of Religion at Florida State University in Tallahassee and earned a PhD in religious studies at FSU. In 1983 he was invited to join the Religious Education faculty at BYU. During his thirty-one years there, he served as chair of the Department of Ancient Scripture, dean of Religious Education, and Richard L. Evans Professor of Religious Understanding.

In 1991, at the strong urging of one of the senior Church leaders, he became involved in interfaith work. In May of 2000 he joined Richard Mouw in organizing the Mormon–Evangelical dialogue. Since then Robert has been involved in academic dialogues with members of Community of Christ (formerly the Reorganized Church of Jesus Christ of Latter Day Saints) and with scholars from the Church of the Nazarene. In addition, he and Richard have been involved in a dialogue with eight Christian scholars, sponsored by the John A. Widtsoe Foundation in Los Angeles, California. It is an honor and a thrill for him to participate with his dear friend and colleague, Richard Mouw, in producing this volume.

Scan the QR code to purchase
and see other books in the
Understanding Our Neighbors Series